Parent Talk

By Willard Abraham, Ph.D.

Home
Study
Collection™
a focus on family learning

Published by
ECS Learning Systems, Inc.
San Antonio, Texas

Library of Congress Cataloging-in-Publication Data

Abraham, Willard.
    Parent talk/by Willard Abraham.
       p.   cm.—(Home study collection)
    ISBN 1-57022-053-0
    1. Preschool children.   2. Education, Preschool—United States.
   3. Child development. I. Title. II. Series.
    HQ774.5.A25   1997
    649.123—dc20

                                              96-41025
                                                CIP

Home
Study
Collection™

a focus on family learning[sm]

Published by
ECS Learning Systems, Inc.
P.O. Box 791437
San Antonio, Texas 78279-1437

ISBN 1-57022-053-0

Printed in the United States of America.

Home Study Collection™ is a trademark of ECS Learning Systems, Inc.

Editors: Lori Mammen and Denise D. Keller, Graphic Designer: Kathleen Magargee

Home Study Collection™ books are available at special discounts for bulk purchases by corporations, institutions, and other organizations. For more information, please contact the Special Sales Department, ECS Learning Systems, Inc., P. O. Box 791437, San Antonio, Texas 78279-1437, 1-800-688-3224.

Table of Contents

Introduction

Your two-year-old isn't interested in toilet training. Your five-year-old still has trouble with certain letter sounds. Your four-year-old is jealous of the new baby. Your only child seems so bright. Are these children normal? What should you do about them?

In this book, you'll find 74 topics offering advice and information on the most important areas of concern to parents and the young children (two to five years old) they love. It covers many vital subjects in an easy-to-use style. Each section stresses an individual topic or concern like gifted children, hyperactivity, discipline and punishment, working mothers, single-parent families. How to select a preschool and guides to determine parental goals are also included.

The early years are much too precious to waste. Through you—the parents—these pleasant, successful approaches can help young children get off to an enjoyable, solid start.

The renowned researcher, Dr. Benjamin S. Bloom of the University of Chicago, stressed the importance of the youthful years "...in terms of intelligence...about 50% of the development takes place between conception and age 4, about 30% between ages 4 and 8, and about 20% between ages 8 and 14...as much of the development takes place in the first 4 years of life as in the next 13 years."

These short, but informative topics are yours to read and re-read, and will help you with your two- to five-year-olds, whether they are the youngest, middle, or eldest children. They will help you learn the important steps parents and their small children take to ensure fulfilling the early growth levels so significant for them.

In general, the ideas and strategies presented in this book would be beneficial in many of the situations you encounter as a parent. But remember, children are individuals, and not all approaches and strategies will be suitable or safe as described herein for you and your child. If you have any questions, you should consult with your child's pediatrician.

A Child's Place in the Family

The Eldest Child

If your preschooler is your first-born child, get ready for problems! That child will become your eldest, and then later you may hear loud comments like these: "What's so special about her? Just because she was born first! She always gets…" Finish it in your own way—the white meat of the chicken, a later bedtime, the chance to see a special movie or an adult TV show. Throughout history the eldest child in the family has been singled out for special attention. Sometimes it was far from a privilege because the first-born boy might have been considered a threat to his father. So he was killed, became a burnt offering, or was devoured as a "solution." The Oedipus myth was one of the most famous examples of a boy taking his father's place. In fairy tales and fiction the first one in the family often stood out. For example, the eldest was given the father's mill in "Puss and Boots," and Meg in *Little Women* showed how great a big sister could be. In many first and second generation families it was assumed that he (sometimes "she," but not as often) would be the best educated, the learned one.

Japanese families assume that the eldest will be favored over others. We may feel or act that way, but most of us never admit it. Fairness and equal opportunity for all of our children—those are the points of view with which we're usually more comfortable.

The eldest frequently seems smarter than the rest (whether or not he or she is), and the reasons should seem obvious. More time is usually available to answer questions, read to him, and take him places. He may have talked earlier and developed a broader vocabulary because of his adult environment. Being a center of attention meant that he generally received plenty of it. He may be more serious, more eager to please, and possibly more selfish than the others. (Watch out! These are generalizations and might appear logical, but perhaps are not even remotely related to your own first born.)

Another common element is resentment against the next ones to come along, those who "displaced" him. Temper, jealousy, and tension might all become the order of the day. He may feel that he has some unfinished business to attend to—the task of completing his own babyhood.

A third item is the responsibility often accepted or placed on those young shoulders. It's not just being responsible for doing things for the others (dressing them, baby-sitting, and diaper-changing, for example), but the hidden one of being held up as a model. School grades, athletic achievement, Boy Scout accomplishments—the list is long and burdensome both to the child and to those who follow. Frequently these pace-setting factors aren't actually mentioned. They don't have to be. They're just there, like the mountain to be climbed.

So many family problems occur because of staggered child arrival. (It obviously would be worse if they all came at once!) How about the younger one who outstrips an older brother or sister in popularity, school success, sports activities, or height? If they're different sexes, there may not be so much difficulty, but if the same sex, then there's even more need to stress the abilities of each, avoid comparisons, and not hold back the advanced one. It is also a good idea to protect the eldest child's seniority factors when it comes to privacy, hours of sleep or study, and other items important to the child.

In many families the first one—as an only, cherished child for a time—should alert us to the problem of child favoritism. It's sometimes a hidden agenda item in the rebellion and antagonisms of those who come later and have difficulty accepting what may seem (or actually be) stronger parent ties of affection and expectation with the elder one.

Do you want to read more on this subject—or leave something around for the other parent who might show partiality for the first born without even knowing it? Locate a copy of a short book by Edith G. Neisser, *The Eldest Child*, published by Harper.

The "Nutcracker" Child . . .
Caught in the Middle

Were you the middle child in your family? Do you now have one of your own? If the answer is "yes" to either of those questions, you may have some definite opinions about what a middle child is like. And your ideas will probably be sound, but only as they pertain to your own youngster. Here is what some parents recently said about theirs.

- "Our middle child is aggressive, angry, a fighter, caught between an older sister and a younger brother."
- "She's withdrawn and reserved; our older and younger ones seem to occupy the center of the stage."
- "Free as a bird, maybe because we had put so many restraints on our first-born and smother the baby with love."

Such aggressive, withdrawn and free-flying traits may, of course, be partly because of the spot a child occupies in the family, but they are related to inherited personality items, too. Another factor concerns parents who aren't always the same, differing in health, income, and attitudes toward each other when different children in the family were the same age. For example, all may have been smooth and easy when the first child was two, but fell apart by the time the second became that age. The tense atmosphere in the second case cannot help but affect how that youngster acts and matures.

And yet, a child *can* be influenced to some extent by his or her position in the family. A middle child seldom has the opportunity for the uninterrupted attention that your first child often received, or the babying that your younger one might get. So the child may have to fight a little harder for recognition.

Relationships depend partly on the sex of the second child, too. If the same as the first, he or she may seem to be an "also-ran," perhaps not quite as eagerly received as one of the other sex might have been. The older one is sometimes held up as an example, by parents as well as by others. How many times did you hear a teacher say something like this: "So you're Mary's little sister? I hope you're as good a student as she was!" Your younger one may seem to be a threat without even trying. Just being there, displacing the next older child, might be enough to build up resentment on the part of the one who came along earlier.

Parents who are unaware of the "nutcracker" possibility of the one caught in the middle sometimes give special attention and show favoritism to help compensate for what they feel is a kind of squeezed position in the family. Or they could ignore the matter, continuing their tendency to cherish the first and last born, leaving the middle one to shift for himself or herself.

Your middle child may have advantages as well as disadvantages. The child might escape the anxious restraints and high expectations imposed on your first born. There may have been an older brother or sister to "break in" your parental skills and anxieties. And the child might avoid the overbearing love and maybe even over-cautious concern you give the third one, the baby.

A second-born child may act as though it's necessary to make up for lost time, striking out for both the rights of the elder and privileges of the younger. One child development expert wrote that "unless he succeeds in pushing himself ahead of his two competitors, he will likely, the rest of his life, hold the conviction that people are unfair to him, that he has no place in the group." It could also be that those "competitors" sometimes close in and form an alliance against the middle child.

Generalizing about this youngster is no more accurate than insisting that all first, youngest, and only children are, respectively, arrogant, pampered, or cherished (although some of them may be, of course). They're different. They all need encouragement and attention. And parents who fully understand the necessity for fair play recognize that family placement really may not matter in the long run. There usually seems to be enough love for all of the children.

"The Last Button on the Coat"
(The youngest child)

The youngest child in the family needs something very special—like being treated as the other children are and receiving recognition in line with his own needs. That's so easy to say and sometimes very difficult to do. Just ask any parent who has more than one child, and you'll begin to see the picture. Their comments may go something like this:

- "I'm more calm with her. Take her in stride better than I did with the others."
- "I worry more. Guess it's because I'm aware of the sicknesses and accidents that can happen to him."
- "...the child of my older age. So cherished and loved."

Although every family and every child are different, there are a lot of truisms that apply to the youngest child (or "the last button on the coat," as one wise man said). She may be spoiled, favored, pampered, and protected. Or your youngest child may even be a bit ignored because you might be less watchful than you were with your first-born, or you have less time because you are now more involved in a job or career, with friends, or in community activities. She may be (or seem) smarter than the older ones because you may talk more to the youngest one, maybe even listen more.

The parents who are sensitive to the possible benefits of having a young child still at home recognize how great a pleasure it can be. The link with youth, the beauty of seeing through a child's eyes, the occasions available to share a youngster's dreams—it's the last time and an opportunity not to be missed or taken lightly. In Rachel Carson's little book, *The Sense of Wonder*, she indicates the chance we have to cling to a child's world as he sees it and the importance of letting him share it with us.

The youngest child in the family still has a hand and mind on things seen and felt for the first time, and it may be our final chance to share a young child's excitement. But taking part in such wonderment doesn't come easily. It may require a few momentary postponements, like temporarily putting off the evening paper, a relaxing social drink, or a phone call, all of them important but perhaps none as enjoyable as what this youngest child has to say if we just give a little time and attention.

Although the youngest child usually brings a lot of enjoyment into the family, there might be problems, too. The youngest may find it comfortable to be "the baby," want to hold on to that special place, and may even be reluctant about growing up and carrying some responsibilities of yard, garbage, dishes, pet care, and money that the older siblings bear. The youngest child may even bring dissension because of the resentment of those who came first.

The youngest one's achievements may not be recognized because although it is the first time for him, you have already gone through scouts, school, hobbies, and all the rest, maybe even more than once. He may have to work very hard to get the attention that older ones obtained so easily.

The youngest child sometimes resembles an only one, especially if there is quite an age difference between him and older brothers and sisters. Then, you face the problem of trying to avoid too much dependence on you or his too frequent involvement with adults. The competition may not be with the siblings but with the parent of the same sex for the affection of the other one.

The most healthful attitude toward the youngest child can be stated quite simply. It is based on answers to questions like these:

- What abilities and needs does the child have?
- How can I best improve and satisfy them?
- What special personality factors require nurturing or correcting?
- What can I do about all of that—and can I afford *not* to face these questions?

It has probably occurred to you that such questions and answers fit into the picture for *all* children, and that's right. The needs of the youngest one are really no different than they are for others in the family. But because the youngest child presents our last chance to help a child grow healthfully, we may have to push ourselves a bit toward meeting them, especially during the important early years.

The Only Child

Do you have an only child in your family? Did you know that only children have often been identified as "different"? Back in 1898, some research said they were below average in health, subject to physical or mental problems, and peculiar. A research study in 1927 agreed. It stated that these children are usually "jealous, selfish, egotistical, dependent, aggressive, domineering, or quarrelsome." (That in itself is almost enough to encourage a second pregnancy or an adoption!)

Then came a study that disagreed with all of that. It stressed their self-confidence and leadership. Another one said these youngsters weren't different at all, although they did seem to be finicky in their food tastes and have temper tantrums more often than other children.

So what's the truth about only children? Although there are, of course, numerous exceptions, these children *are* sometimes handicapped in their adjustment to others. They may be limited in their opportunities to play and compete with other children and sheltered from the normal give-and-take of childhood. They are more often caught in a bind simply because there are no other children for parents to watch, nag, and love. The importance of a good preschool program may, therefore, be pretty obvious to you.

If you are the parent of an only child, you may tend toward being overly protective, as often happens with the first born. This attitude could exist because only children are occasionally born to older parents or to those who want but can't have any others. So you may worry over small illnesses, praise them too much for doing little things, and interfere too often. A headache, a star on an ordinary school paper, an invitation to another youngster's birthday party may become too big a thing. The early involvement of many of these children with adults might lead to other children disliking them. After all, who wants to play with a child who uses big words and seems to think he's better than the rest?

Some of the problem times for only children are when they go to school for the first time (others also may cling to mother, but perhaps not as much), bedtime with too many books and records and maybe lying down with the youngster for too long, and mealtimes with coaxing and catering to food fads and whims. Such situations occur in other families, of course, but might take place more frequently when there's an only child.

Only children often have a lot of advantages. There could be more money for education, toys, and clothes when there is only one child to spend it on. Parents have more time for one than for many, and there may also be more vacations and travel. Because of such advantages, only children might seem brighter than other children, reflecting the time and enrichment given to them.

Most parents of only children know they could have a problem on their hands, and sometimes work hard to avoid it. Nursery school and summer camps if the family budget permits, having other youngsters come to visit as much as possible, and broadening their own interests and activities are all good practices to consider. It's better for the child if the parents get involved in their own music, art, or school or college courses, anything productive and unrelated to the youngster. The child will probably get plenty of attention anyway.

The possible difficulties are sometimes made worse by grandparents if they have only one grandchild. There could be similar problems if there's only one boy among a group of sisters, or just one girl among boys. Any situation where pampering may occur requires being careful to keep the youngster from dominating the family.

An only child may be lonely and dependent—but could just as well be the most popular child on the block. It all depends on the child's personality and how well the parents balance their love and concern with an awareness that they can give and do too much.

Only children may be no more selfish or hard to get along with than children in larger families. They may be no brighter. Just like the oldest, youngest, disabled, or hyperactive, they are children first.

A New Baby at Your House

"What is the single most difficult part of your work?" I recently asked a busy pediatrician. With no hesitation he replied, "The new baby. Not its health, care, or feeding, but what to do about an older brother or sister. Especially if that one is young, a preschooler."

"You mean the new baby can be even more of a problem than sickness or accidents?"

"The new baby isn't the problem, usually far from it. But his or her presence brings changes, adjustments. It is often difficult for parents to understand them, especially when there is another young child already at home. Sometimes they don't even know they have a problem. They may be too busy adjusting to the new child and to their own new life to notice."

"Notice what?"

"Jealousy, for example. It comes out in different ways. Back to the bottle, baby talk, a sucked thumb, wetting or getting messed up, moping around, saying the baby should go back to the hospital, or even hitting the baby."

"So what should parents do when there's an older one at home?"

His advice, combined with the ideas of others concerned about this kind of rivalry, added up to these suggestions:

- Prepare the way well in advance, by moving the older child into a new room, bigger bed, enrolling him in a good preschool. Change the older child's life as little as possible, especially right after the baby is born.
- Let the new father carry the baby into the house for the first time so that the mother is free to talk, laugh, and play with your waiting preschool child.
- Try to restrain father, grandparents, and friends from gushing over the new baby when the older one is around. You might even have some small presents for the older child when visitors bring gifts for the baby.

- Realize it is normal for a young child (and the rest of us, too!) to be jealous, to fear, to resent. Such attitudes cannot be completely prevented. No one likes to see his place taken by someone else, whether it is a new child—or a new husband or wife!
- Appeal to the older one's desire to grow up by giving responsibilities that can be handled and compliments that are deserved. Remember that 1) two- to five-year-olds are still young and immature, capable of completing only small, short-term tasks, and 2) fake, undeserved praise is phony and easy for them to see through.
- Turn rivalry into helpfulness. "Help me"…with feeding, bathing, dressing. "Give me"…a towel, bottle, diaper. "Hold the baby"…when there is no danger of dropping.
- Accept the older child's feelings, but not necessarily the actions. First, the baby is to be protected. Second, let your older one know that you recognize how she feels…may wish the baby weren't there…likes to hear "I love you very much," accompanied by reassuring smiles and hugs.
- Realize that you can bend over too far in comforting the older one. You have no reason to feel guilty or insecure. Although babies need attention and affection, too, they require less time during the early months and can often be cared for, to some extent, when the other isn't there.
- Try not to appear surprised or shocked by what the older child does, or to shame the older child for showing normal feelings. If you do, they may be driven "underground," and then harder to deal with. If you either ignore or accept them, they probably won't last long anyway.

A new baby in the family can be a good learning experience for all its members, but it's tough on a little boy or girl who was an only child or the youngest one until then. However, the experience can help teach a lesson we all should learn sometime: To share love and time; to accept conflict and rivalry; to realize no one can always have his or her own way. A baby can be quite a teacher for older brothers or sisters who are still close to being babies themselves. Just being around the little one helps the others grow up.

Brothers and Sisters
Getting Along Together

Quarreling…teasing…yelling at each other…this is the normal situation in most families. Even preschoolers get involved in what seems like a never-ending race to be first, to have the last word, and to get hold of a toy (especially if it belongs to a brother or sister). Some of your friends may tell you that their children always get along well together. They never argue or fight, really love one another. But they are probably not seeing their children as they really are or they have unusual children.

Most brothers and sisters are in competition with each other. The closer they are in age, the more they compete for your affection and approval—and the more they may show resentment when you do something for one and not for the rest. Young children have an especially difficult time. They may not yet have learned the skill of sharing and "taking turns," or the fun there is in giving as well as receiving.

Some conflict among children can be prevented. Much of it takes place when they are tired, hungry, or bored. Touchy periods also occur when they are forced to spend too much time together. Irritants like shared closets, radios, and toys aren't always necessary. Even a major period of stress, like when a new baby comes, can be planned for so that a preschooler doesn't feel displaced or rejected. A little preparation can keep the youngster from asking inwardly, "Wasn't I good enough?"

Sharing the news a few weeks ahead of time, making room changes or preschool arrangements before the baby comes, using the young child as a helper with the baby, and expecting the child to slip back into babyish habits (without punishment or ridicule from you) are among the ways you can ease both of you through this period.

A few basic rules of parental common sense can help reduce rivalry among your children:

- Recognize that each child is different. You may give one more time because she requires it, another more compliments (but only earned ones) because she needs them, and a third a particular book, a paint set, or a ball and bat because she will make good use of them.
- Understand that children's relationships are affected by their age, place in the family, and sex, as well as by their appearance, personality, interests, and abilities. For example, the youngest has never been an only child (the oldest was), the middle one is kind of closed in, and one girl among boys (or a boy among girls) is in a position different from all the rest.
- Avoid comparisons. They merely add to possible conflict and tension.
- Make each child special in some way. All children need to feel important, and parents are the best ones to satisfy that need. A good preschool can also help in creating a secure, happy self-image.
- Develop a fair pattern of seniority. Older brothers and sisters may get the comics first and stay up later, but all have to share responsibilities in line with their maturity (taking out the garbage, straightening up their rooms, caring for pets, and other family chores). However, young children can receive special attention; they may be the only ones read to, played with, and taken to the grocery store, all events that are fun for them.
- Encourage respect among all of them (and on your part, too) for their privacy and possessions. Even the youngest deserves uninterrupted time to finish a game or build a block castle.
- Keep out of disagreements unless one is always getting the worst of it, and even then only when you know all sides of the problem.
- Realize that all's not lost, not when they are able to present a united front in planning a birthday surprise for you, pull together against the bully down the block, or boast of each other's accomplishments.
- Let their feelings come out, even if they are sometimes noisy. It's better than forcing their resentment and jealousy underground. Let them know their attitudes are normal, just as the ways in which younger ones admire and imitate and older ones protect and teach are normal.

Perhaps the most important factor related to childhood family rivalry is this: The love and hate, fun and quarrels, and help and hurt are the best foundation for the compromises, adjustments, and competition we all have to face throughout our lives.

Parents and Other Role Models

Your Young Child's Most Important Teacher—You

You may not see yourself as a teacher, or want to be or feel prepared to be one—but you are. In fact, you are the only continuous teacher during your child's period of most rapid growth (birth to five years old), and you are the only person to teach your child on a one-to-one basis.

A famous educator said that children "learn by doing." That's true, but they also learn by watching, copying, listening, and talking, and that is where you come in. Many of your own activities can be shared with your preschool child. While cooking there are words to use like "mix," "taste," "stir," "turn," and more complicated ones like "season" and "simmer." In laundry work there are sorting, matching, and folding activities. Car tires need air, grass needs watering, tables must be set for meals—the list is long, and *both* parents can add to it. They can also help break down the sex patterns that once made children think what happened in the home was "women's work," and "men's work" was something entirely different.

A young child points at things, but you can give names to the flowers, foods, and clothing that the child sees. A horse "gallops," a plant "blossoms," a friend comes to "visit," and there are so many other ways to help little children learn the Who, What, When, Where, Why, and How of this large, exciting world of theirs. Helping your youngster hear and use new words and see new places, people, and products is part of your role as a teacher. It doesn't take a lot of time or money, very little in fact. It does require remembering, once in a while, how important you are in your young child's life, now and for the future.

The child asks questions, and you can answer them (as long as your patience lasts!)—but you can ask questions about what happened at preschool or at home during the day. You may have to remind yourself that a child wants to know what *you* did during all those hours you were apart. *Your work*, the trip to and from there, the people you saw, and what they said and you said, did, and thought. It can have a lot more learning in it than the old lines, "Where did you go?" "What did you do?" and the answers of "Out" and "Nothing."

A child learns alone through play and toys, but a few minutes out of your busy day are wanted and enjoyed, too. That precious time together requires some knowledge of what a "normal" two- to five-year-old is like. To expect more than your child can do may make her feel like a failure, a disappointment to you. For example, the speech of young children is *not* perfect, their attention span *is* usually short, and they need *your approval*. It can't be a happy time if you are too tired, worried, or upset to enjoy it as well as to show an honest interest in what you are doing together. Any good preschool teacher can give you valuable suggestions on how to use these times well. They may relate to sock puppets, paper-bag masks, old games like "Simon Says," and new ones based on counting and matching.

Just a bit of caution in closing—if you feel your parent-as-teacher activity is getting too serious, too rigid, or in the way of having a good time as a *parent*, forget it. It's not worth one minute of pressure or feeling that it should all be somebody else's job. If it reaches that point, you've worked too hard at teaching your young child. It's then time to "loosen up," relax, and enjoy being "just a parent" again.

YOU are Number 1!

You've sat up nights, bleary-eyed, to nurse a two-year-old through a high fever, diarrhea, and painful teething. You have been ready to steer your car over a cliff because of the screaming, spilled milk, and smells of traveling with young children. You worry about the scare figures of what it will cost to send them to college. You put them first, ahead of yourself, in planning a vacation, scheduling meals, or deciding what you will do next weekend.

Some parents like to be self-sacrificing, to be able to tell themselves (and perhaps others) how much they have done for their children. It may make them feel good to see the furniture they have bought or made for them, the meals especially prepared for them, the new clothing they wear, and the swimming or other lessons arranged for them. They may feel even more pleased about all these if concern for their own furniture, meals, clothing, and bridge or music lessons are put off to some distant future time. Your young children deserve your *time, attention, concern,* and *love,* of course. But at least once in a while, all four of those factors should be aimed in another direction—toward you.

As important as our children are to us, it's time to think about "Number 1." A little more emphasis on yourself may actually help make you an even better parent than you are now. It will also contribute to your enjoyment as you see the months and years of your own youth slip by so quickly.

- *Your relationship with your husband (or wife).* How often have the demands of your youngsters interfered with a conversation or a quiet time you were having together? Did they really have to be met at that moment—or was what you were doing more important? Have your and your spouse's attitudes on how to handle a young child differed to the point of arguing over them? Was it all worth the anger you felt toward each other?

- *Money.* Are there times when you haven't even thought about dollars for your own clothing, movies, vacations, or restaurant meals?
- *Time.* Did you take your preschool child somewhere because it was "so good for him"—shopping, to see a train, or to view an ice show—when the child couldn't have cared less, and you were tired or you wanted to see a "four-star" movie or a ball game instead? Have you ever thought that they have so much more time now and in the future than you do?
- *Gifts.* Have you considered the amount of money and effort you spend on buying Christmas, birthday, and other presents for them, maybe much more than you do for each other or for yourself?

One writer gave parents something to think about with these words concerning those without children:

There is nothing sadder than the childless couple. It breaks your heart to see them stretched out relaxing around swimming pools in Florida, sitting all sun-tanned and miserable on the decks of their boats, trotting off to Europe like lonesome fools. It is an empty life. There is nothing but more money to spend, and more time to enjoy it.

The poor childless couple gets so selfish and wrapped up in their own concerns that you have to feel sorry for them. They can't fight over a child's discipline, can't blame each other for the child's nauseous characteristics, and they miss all the fun of doing without for the child's sake. They go along from day to day doing what they want, buying what they want, and liking each other. It is a pretty pathetic picture.

Wet mattresses, doctor bills, temper tantrums, and you can add other crises you've struggled through—these are the other side of the picture. Yes, young children bring joy along with tears, yelling, and frayed nerves. A hug, a laugh, and the first words and steps will all become precious memories. But now, right now, today, you have to come first sometimes…what you will do tonight, shop for to eat, put on, or how will you use that next vacation. Our pampering of them should sometimes be directed toward us. We deserve it!

They're Watching You!

Some experts who study family relationships come up with fancy words that describe them—for example, the "role" a parent takes or the "model" the parent provides as an example for children. More important than those words is the fact that for many years, especially during the early ones, you are the center of attention, the most important person in your young child's life. What you say, how you look at the child, and what you do are listened to and watched. Those small eyes and ears miss very little. What they see and hear is the basis of what kind of people they will grow up to be.

Here is a checklist of ten items that you might think about once in a while. It may be that you really don't want to be the type of person they represent, but at least they will help you understand what your preschool-age child is looking at.

Do you want your child to—

- *Be honest?* Then perhaps it's time to stop nibbling the grapes and shelling a peanut or two as you go through the supermarket. Even though young children may not understand what's involved in a false insurance claim and taking home paper, pens, and tape from your office (and talking about such practices), they can get the impression that dishonesty is "normal" and maybe even an all-right thing to practice.
- *Like to read?* When did *you* last read a book all the way through or read one to and with your youngster? What example do you set in the time you devote to reading, and how apparent is your enjoyment of it?
- *Develop neat habits?* Do you pick up after yourself, put things away, and take pride in some order, whether it relates to planning meals, making beds, or driving a clean car?

- *Show affection?* Within our families we sometimes neglect to show affection through hugs, kisses, smiles, and saying nice things. It is far from a sign of weakness for the boys and men in the family also to show their feelings.
- *Have respect for other people?* As adults we too often interrupt, cut off, or ignore our young children, or show disrespect for their privacy and possessions. It may be hard for us to realize that they, too, deserve at least some of the regard that we often show for complete strangers. And who's more important anyway?
- *Use words correctly?* The words we use and how we use them set the example for our children. They quote us, copy us, and feel that what we say must be acceptable. But it's kind of unpleasant sometimes to hear *our* words come from *their* mouths!
- *Complete tasks?* Why should they, if our unfinished housework, letter writing, dirty dishes, and job activities are daily reminders that adults often have a lot of loose ends in their lives? We usually want them to stick to tasks and respect deadlines, but they might not unless we also do so.
- *Listen to what others say?* If we are so busy talking that we fail to respect, or even hear, the ideas of others, we hardly provide a good example for them. Many of us have such a desire to impose our ideas on children that we don't even realize they have ideas, too.
- *Be sincere in human relationships?* Fake friendships, talking about people behind their backs, smiling but not with our eyes—it's on such a foundation that insincere relationships are based. And they are learned about in the first few years of life.
- *Set up priorities and show moderation toward them?* Our own TV watching, eating, drinking, smoking, and sleeping habits certainly don't go unnoticed. What is important to us is often important to them, so perhaps we should take some care in what priorities we set up in our own lives, for our own benefit as well as theirs.

A wise person once said that the apple doesn't fall far from the tree. If we're satisfied with the image we provide, then that's a comfortable thought to live with. But if we're not, then what? As the current saying goes, the ball is in your court.

What Kind of Parent am I?

"How effective am I as a parent?" Do you ever ask yourself that question? Perhaps you do, and your answer may be "So-so," "Pretty bad," or perhaps "Great!" Here is a self-rating scale that may help you look at yourself a little more objectively. It will just take a few minutes to complete. Rate yourself on each item: Good—2 points; Fair—1 point; Poor—0; I don't know—3. (Circle your answer.)

- *Communication.* Young children try to use a lot of words, but not always accurately. Nor are they always easy to understand. But correcting them isn't as important as listening, exchanging ideas, and actually carrying on a conversation. Do I let them tell me what they did at their day care center or preschool? Do we have some "Talking Time" every day? Do I answer their question, in words they can understand? 2 1 0 3
- *Time.* Merely spending time together is less important than enjoying or laughing at things together. Do we really like each other's company? Do I regularly take time for playing a game, taking a walk, going to the park, or seeing a movie with my preschool child? 2 1 0 3
- *Example.* Children learn by copying their parents. Do I set a good example by following through on my job, being honest in my relationships, and showing moderation in my TV watching, drinking, eating, sleeping, and other habits? Nibbling grapes from the supermarket fruit bin may seem like such a small thing, but it's too important to be seen by a young child. What kind of example do I set in controlling my temper and moodiness? 2 1 0 3
- *Expectations and responsibilities.* Are the expectations I have for my children realistic...or too high or low? Do they help with the dishes, make beds, pick up clothes, and do other home chores of which they are

capable? Do I add to their duties gradually? Is my preschool child beginning to understand money and what things cost?   2   1   0   3

- *Praise.* Do I use praise, or just nag? Do I notice and reward (even with a
  kind word) what my young child does, whether it's something small like
  taking out the garbage or a big achievement like reading his first word
  in a book?   2   1   0   3
- *Limitations.* Do our family rules fit the age and abilities of my children?
  Do I set limits that make sense for each child, like a time frame for
  going to bed or the amount of TV watching permitted? But do I also
  realize that there has to be some flexibility in schedules, to help children
  adjust to change?   2   1   0   3
- *Reading.* Do my young children see me reading, and do I read to them?
  Is it fun for them and me? Do we choose the books together and have a
  good time talking about them? How often do I go to the library with
  them?   2   1   0   3
- *Strengths and weaknesses.* Do I make an effort to see my children as
  they really are, not as I'd like them to be? Do I accept the fact that they
  may not be as good-looking and clever as I sometimes think they are?
  Am I aware of their limitations, as in catching a ball, cutting with
  scissors, skipping, or hopping? If they are lagging behind others, am I
  doing something about it?   2   1   0   3
- *Discipline.* If we are a two-parent family, do we agree on approaches to
  discipline? Do we stick together in our ideas so that our children can't
  play one of us against the other? If I'm the only parent, am I consistent
  in the discipline I use? Do I try to prevent problems by keeping medicines, candy, and valuable breakable things away from little hands?
  2   1   0   3
- *Love.* It's the most important factor of all. Do I try to show it through
  buying them everything they ask for...or in more important ways like
  hugs, touching, smiles, quiet talk, and saying nice things?   2   1   0   3

How did you do? A perfect score would be 20. If you ended up with 16 to 20
points, that may sound fine—but one failed item may be enough to mess up
your whole relationship. For example, if you never use praise or use it dis-
honestly, or think that showing your love is a sign of weakness, it may not
matter at all how well you did on the others.

Still, a high score...and a low score, too...may tell you something about
your parental effectiveness. These items can also be a guide toward a better
understanding of your youngster, and of yourself. And a lot of points in the "I
don't know" column say something important to you, too, like, "Maybe it's
time to think more about the young child in my family."

The "Pushy" Parent

"Stage mothers" aren't all in the theater or movies. They don't all have (or work hard to have) talented children like Shirley Temple. They are also on the tennis courts, in the school principal's office, and at little league games. Nor are they all mothers. Plenty of fathers get into the act, too.

Have you ever stood next to a new father gazing into a hospital nursery and heard him say, "He'll make it! He'll be a doctor! Doesn't he look smart?" Or perhaps you know parents who talk about their young child's tapered fingers, good coordination, or ability with numbers, and know that they are thinking about a future pianist, dancer, or accountant.

We all have dreams for our young children. We want them to be healthy, happy, and successful. But such desires can be either unrealistic because the youngster just doesn't have the appropriate ability or dangerous because we may really be thinking more of our own unfulfilled hopes than their future happiness.

"I never made it to law school, but he will, that's for sure," represents a common thought, although not usually expressed quite so openly. In fact, the parental pressure is often subtle, even unknowingly applied. It takes place not only with what children will do in their job future, but also in how they will look and act. Actress Bette Davis told the story of the mother and daughter who visited her after she had made the movie *Now Voyager*. (You might recall her role of the mild, dowdy daughter of a demanding, oppressive mother.) "How un-realistic!" the visiting mother said. "No one would do that to their child." And there, right next to her, was her own daughter, plain and meek, an exact copy of Bette Davis' film character.

"*We* won the Science Fair contest" or "*We* became an Eagle Scout" brags the pushy parent. The parent is so deeply ingrained in the child's accomplishment that it interferes with the pleasure of achievement being where it really belongs. All this pleasure can begin early, in those important first few years.

As a parent of a young child you might check yourself on times like these:

- Do you assume that your child has certain interests, like dolls or tractors, just because the child is a girl or boy? (Try not to assume anything. A little careful observation can tell you what the child really enjoys.)
- Do you lavishly praise every small thing your youngster does, when you know that the finger painting actually is nothing to rave about? (Deserved praise makes more sense.)
- Do you use "when" not "if" as you talk about your child's career (the "Dictionary of Occupational Titles" of the U.S. Bureau of Labor Statistics lists thousands of occupations, and there are countless changing and new ones. So what's the hurry?)
- Do you fail to get hints from your young child that some of those lessons where you drag him are perhaps both unpleasant and worthless? (You want to expose your youngster to what you perhaps never had—but which ones and how many and how often?)
- Do you frequently talk about what you might have done or money you would have earned if only you had gone to college or worked for a higher degree? (There is implied pressure in such comments.)

If you answer "Yes" to any of these questions, perhaps you have a problem and are creating another for your child. And yet, there's another side to the story. Without a parent's support, interest, and enthusiasm, a child may not reach the goals for which she is well-equipped. It takes careful observation for a parent to accurately notice a child's interests and capabilities. It also takes restraint to guide rather than push. And finally, it is a fulfillment of *their* hopes, not ours, that should be the target for our children's future happiness.

Are You a Working Mother?

- "I'm working and have very little time to spend with my children. After all, when I get home, there's dinner to make and washing, ironing, and cleaning to do."
- "How much am I hurting my children by going to work?"

You may not be hurting them at all. In fact, taking a job may be the best thing you can do for them. Enjoying your work, making extra money, and feeling good about yourself are all important factors for the working mother to consider. Two jobs in the family often make the difference between skimpy and satisfying meals, not having or having at least a short summer vacation, and TV dinners and TV watching at night instead of eating out once in a while and an occasional night on the town.

For single mothers the job may be even more necessary than when there is another paycheck coming in. But for them, too, the nagging question may keep coming up: "What am I doing to my young children by being away so much?"

Most working mothers should feel no guilt at all about taking jobs, according to some research on this subject. In fact, it often indicates that many mothers who have to or want to work should obtain both pride and pleasure from the fact that they can do two jobs well, one at home and the other outside. Dr. Lois Wladis Hoffman at the University of Michigan found that—

- When mothers like their jobs, their attitudes rub off on their children. They help make their home a happier place.
- Daughters of working mothers have a more modern, open view of women's place in the world than do girls whose mothers are limited to managing the home.

- Working away from home doesn't seem to deprive school-age children of much, if anything.
- Many working mothers tend to have a false picture of the non-working mother-child relationship. The at-home mother may not use her time to read to children, play games with them, and take them places as much as the one who works may imagine.

Just because you are employed doesn't necessarily mean you will spend less time with your youngsters. Your good sense or guilt feelings, or both, may encourage you to use the early morning, evening, and weekend hours more carefully and waste them less than a mother who is there all the time. Planned activities, a Saturday afternoon movie together, before-bedtime reading, enjoying togetherness in watching a TV program—these may be a regular part of your schedule. You are more likely to plan your time carefully and guard closely the limited number of hours you have at home. However, you also have to guard against too many presents and treats, like candy and ice cream, just because you have a job and less time for your youngsters.

Whether you work or not isn't the key point in your children's development anyway. Far more important are items that may not be related to your job situation at all. A checklist like this one indicates matters of more importance in your child's growth and adjustment:

- Do parents get along well with each other?
- Do they like what they do with most of their waking hours, whether inside or outside the home?
- If only one lives in the home, is that parent adjusted to single "blessedness"?
- Is some time scheduled with each child alone, the amount of it related to the youngster's needs?
- Are the common-sense attitudes of non-favoritism, discipline, and love (shown through words, touching, holding, and kissing) used with all?
- Do your young children attend a preschool whose personnel and program you have checked into thoroughly?

Going to work or not isn't the major factor in the relationships we have with our children. How we feel about our lives and theirs, and how we show such feelings are more vital. Although we started out talking about working mothers, most of what's been said also applies to their fathers, of course.

The Man in Your Young Child's Family

Every young child needs a man in the family. Most little children have one. If there isn't a father, it might be necessary to bring in someone else. Grandfathers, uncles, cousins, older brothers, or adult male friends may have to be the father-substitute. Modern preschools and day care centers try to hire men as teachers or teacher aides. So far few have entered this field, however, so the masculine contact generally has to come at home. It's important for both little boys and girls. They get a strange view of the world around them if they see only women earning a living, paying bills, and running the house. Even if their mother reads to them, plays with them, and answers most of their questions, young children still miss something they need very much.

Just any adult male can't fill the gap. He should be one they can look up to and admire, and whose strength and gentleness both come through to them. But merely "being around" isn't enough either. He must get involved with them, in what they do, think, and say. His tasks can be fun, are not difficult, and don't require much time. The man in your child's family can check himself on these eight factors to see how well he is doing.

- When did you last sit on the floor with the youngster? How often do you do it?
- What do you do with the child when you're there? Is it something about which she is excited, that she enjoys and talks about, and in which she wants you to take part?
- Do you listen to him? Do you share your ideas with him so he can understand them? Do you respond to his ideas in words that are clear to him? Do you talk in full sentences?

- What do you do when you first come home from work (or if you're not the father, when you first come in)? For those few minutes, are you willing to put off looking at the newspaper or television and talking to other adults, giving the child your full attention? The first five minutes are often more important to young children than all the rest of the evening hours put together.
- Are you willing to let the child help you with some of your own jobs around the house? Maybe it will take a few minutes longer that way, but do you let her help fix the faucet, put a battery in a flashlight, or cut the grass? Do you discuss with her what you're doing while you do it?
- How often do you spend time alone with one child, with no other children or adults around? It needn't be a long involvement either, maybe just as simple as taking a walk around the block with him or taking him to the store with you.
- Do you ever hold her hand, let her sit on your lap, hug her, or kiss her? It's far from being a sign of weakness to touch children. You'll like it, and most of them do, too.
- Does it bother you that little boys sometimes play with dolls and little girls like to use tools to fix and make things? It isn't really necessary that preschoolers know about some of the sex roles they may fill later on. Doing what's "expected" will probably come in time anyway. Boys and girls may not require certain roles; others might react to modern attitudes of children with similar goals.

Whenever possible, the man/child relationship should begin in the earliest months and continue on a regular basis during the preschool years (and later). If it becomes a special thing—like once a month—it can't be a natural, normal part of a little child's life. Fathers and adult male substitutes set an example for young children. The little eyes and ears see and hear everything they do. They learn so much by imitating. The man in your child's family is an important teacher, and it may sometimes be necessary to remind him of that fact. Then, remind him again—and again—how much his little boy or girl needs at least a little of his time, attention, and love.

The Single-Parent Family

Mother, father, and home are the young child's whole world. But neither divorce nor separation will necessarily destroy it. The single parent has to hold it together, and most parents left to live alone with one or more children have all that is needed to create a well-adjusted, healthy family unit. Although the religious factor dominates this situation for some people, for most their personal desires, needs, and "How will our children be affected?" take top consideration.

Having two parents around is important, but it's not essential. More significant may be the fact that tension, hostility, or indifference might also leave when one parent walks out. That closing door may even bring a sense of relief, with quiet and peacefulness at home for the first time.

There are all kinds of "broken homes," and whether yours is really wrecked, temporarily cracked, or perhaps even more solid depends on the strength of the parent left behind, the help of family and friends, and the ability to ease children through the change. It also depends on how well the practical burdens of money, sickness, and discipline are handled. (Separation through death of a parent often provides additional emotional burdens, of course.)

A preschool child living with one parent is frequently troubled inwardly. "I did it...they blame me...they don't love me" are feelings that can lead to anger, fear, and resentment. Children may not actually say these things, but they could feel them deeply. The feelings sometimes surface through hard-to-handle eating; sleeping and bathroom habits; fights with brothers, sisters, and friends; biting and scratching; and belligerence toward naps and other routines that ran so smoothly until the family broke up. How well your young child adjusts to the separation can relate to your using approaches like these:

- Recognize that keeping the separation secret, once it is firmly decided, merely increases anxiety and puzzlement. A small child doesn't need much time to accept an empty place at mealtime.
- Help the child see that she wasn't the reason for it, that it's between two adults, and not because of her. It is important for her to realize that you both love her, so say it and show it.
- As much as possible control any bitterness you may feel, so that the child's distress can be reduced at least a little bit. A young child is very sensitive to bickering, loud arguments, and long silences. He can't handle them in loneliness and fear.
- Try to keep alive her love for the other parent.
- Don't use your child as an emotional outlet or as a "replacement." "You're now the man of the house" may be satisfying and flattering at first, but children shouldn't be expected to provide a substitute for adult affection and companionship to fill the single parent's empty hours. If you need an outlet, seek another adult.
- Recognize that more time and listening may be necessary, but don't assume you have to carry this responsibility so far that friends and hobbies must be restricted or eliminated. You need them, too.

If you have to move, let your youngster keep as many familiar toys and possessions as possible. And if you're getting ready to remarry, realize that children need time to "make friends" with a new parent.

One of the most valuable sources of help to the single-parent family that includes a young child is a competently run nursery school or preschool. It's vital to check out its personnel, program, and facilities. If you tell the staff about your situation, they can help compensate for whatever family deficiencies might exist. People to love, friends the child needs, and toys and large equipment are all available there.

Your adjustment rubs off on your children. If you can live comfortably within your budget, be satisfied with your job, and adapt to being single reasonably well, you generally have little to worry about as far as your youngsters are concerned. They can accept both change and sacrifice when the need is obvious, and when you set the example of taking things in stride.

Grandparents Love
Little Children, Too

It isn't only parents who love and are concerned about young children. Sometimes in the shadows, sometimes right in the middle are their grandparents. Still not fully understood nor accepted is their new role, so different from the one most of us remember about our own grandparents. Then they were regularly in our house or we were in theirs down the street. Some of our children still have that closeness, of course, but not many of them. Most of us recognize how much all of us lose by the distance that separates families. The very special kind of affection that comes naturally to most grandparents isn't available for all children these days. And there is just no substitute for it. Letters, birthday and holiday gifts, and brief visits including short conversations, lunches together, and trips to the ice cream store are thin alternatives for being a deep part of each other's lives.

Other changes have taken place, too. Grandparents often retain their youth and live longer than they used to. They frequently have the energy and enthusiasm it takes to be happy with young children. When they are family visitors, rather than closely knit family members, the old baby-sitting and help-with-housework roles are less common. They may stay with the youngsters once in a while, but not on a regular basis. "Let me enjoy the visit—you raise your own family (I've already raised mine)—I'll try to deserve your and their respect, knowing I can't demand it." These are key feelings of many modern grandparents.

The rare love they have for their grandchildren is sometimes accompanied by conflicts caused by two generations with different beliefs. Children can get caught between the child-rearing opinions of their parents and grandparents related to discipline, bedtime hours, toilet training, and meal schedules. Dad and Grandpa may disagree, for example, on when a boy should get a bike.

The easy solution to suggest (but not necessarily enforce) is that "we may have different points of view, but they all make sense." Such differences may provide a learning experience for youngsters, proving that people have varying ideas, all or most of which can be "right."

A grandfather who partially replaces the absent father in the single-parent family and mothers and daughters-in-law creating discomfort for children because of their hidden or not-so-hidden rivalry for the man of the house are two additional conflict points. When one has lived a long time, it is difficult not to give advice and to let the younger generations (children and grandchildren) make their own mistakes. It's just as difficult not to reject that advice when no one asked for it in the first place. Patience and even silent, uncomfortable restraint may be necessary on both sides.

Perhaps humor is the best way to look at part of this child-adult relationship which can be so rich and warm. A third-grader at W. Alexander School in Oakland, California, put it this way, about one kind of grandmother (Her article entitled "What is a Grandmother?" appeared in "Volunteer Viewpoints," published by the Washington Technical Institute in Washington, D.C.).

A grandmother is a lady who has no children of her own. She likes other people's little girls. A grandfather is a man grandmother. He goes for walks with boys and they talk about fishing and tractors and things like that.

Grandmas don't have to do anything except be there. They are so old they shouldn't run. It is enough if they drive us to the market where "The Pretend Horse" is and have lots of dimes, or if they take us for a walk, and slow down past things like pretty leaves or caterpillars. They should never say "hurry up."

Usually they are fat, but not too fat to tie your shoes. They wear glasses and funny underwear. They can take their teeth and gums off. It is better if they don't typewrite or play cards except with us.

They don't have to be smart, only answer questions like "Why do dogs hate cats?" or "How come God isn't married?" They do not talk baby talk like visitors do because it is hard to understand.

When they read to us they don't skip over anything or mind if it is the same story again. Everybody should try to have one, especially if you don't have a television, because Grandmas are the only grown-ups who have got time.

What Can You Expect?

How Realistic are You About Your Young Child?

No one expects a blind child to see—or a deaf child to hear—or a severely involved cerebral palsied child to walk with a smooth, even step. But parental expectations of other youngsters may be completely unrealistic.

"She must have a speech problem," concluded the mother. "Otherwise why would she say 'yady' for 'lady' and 'wan' for 'ran'?"

Faulty expectations. It is important for parents to know what is "normal," what can be expected in speech patterns of children at various ages. For example, the "l" and "r" sounds come late and so do others like "th," "s," and "v." When parents expect too early what will evolve later, they may be asking for disappointment and unnecessary concern.

Another parent expressed this worry. "He's 16 months old and not walking yet. Do you think he may have a muscular problem? Or maybe there's brain damage. Cerebral palsy or mental disability."

A little knowledge of the causes, prevention, and results of handicapping conditions can be a dangerous thing. Here's a parent who knows that most children walk earlier than 16 months, but who doesn't realize that some well within the normal range take off on their feet later on. This particular baby was unusually heavy, the first child in the family, with every desire of his immediately satisfied. In fact, they labeled him "The Great Pointer" because that forefinger pointing toward any toy or food brought the desired object to him. For him walking expectations were unrealistic. He didn't have any "felt need."

How about this viewpoint concerning a bright boy not working very hard in school? "He does what is expected of him, at home and in school, but he's capable of so much more. He's so smart, you know."

This parent was then asked, "Do either of you or his teachers expect him to work beyond his grade level, read books higher up the ladder, stretch his reasoning in math, science, or anything else?" The parent thought for a moment, and then replied, "No, I don't suppose so. He's happy in school and doing as well as the other kids. After all, he is working up to his grade level, so I guess we really shouldn't expect more of him."

Actually they should, because the gifted child who slovenly moves along at a level beneath his capabilities could easily become dissatisfied with school. Not that nagging and pushing are in order, of course, but a realistic understanding of what his capabilities are, and of performance expectations consistent with them, can help avoid those school frustrations.

In contrast with questionable expectations based on speech patterns for which a child isn't ready, mobility beyond his development, and performance beneath his intellectual levels, other parents have derived almost ecstatic satisfaction because their expectations were exceeded by children with handicapping conditions. The father of a mentally challenged boy (somewhere between 25 and 50 IQ) shared his pleasure in this way:

"Whenever I visited him at the institution, I took him down to the corner drugstore for an ice cream soda. For years we followed that routine. And one day he did it. He actually drank through the straw. The feeling I had was more satisfying than hearing that our bright eighth-grade daughter passed a tough examination in high school algebra or our fifth grader read *David Copperfield*."

An understanding of children's capabilities and limitations, and a realistic view of what to expect, should be based on seeing children as they really are—not as we would like them to be, not as we view them in comparison with other children in our own family, but as they are in their own development and in a setting where there are other children. Teachers can help us be realistic. So can pediatricians, scout leaders, and others who work with children. They can encourage us to stop yanking a child in a direction for which he or she is not ready, or to steer the child into activities that we may have discouraged for too long.

Boys and Girls— And What to Expect

- Little boys playing house and with dolls, crying, showing their concern and feelings toward others…
- Little girls climbing trees, hammering, playing baseball, putting together mechanical things…

When parents worry about young boys doing "feminine" things and pre-school girls interested in "boyish" activities, they may be behind the times. Many activities that people recognize as either male or female overlap these days. Look at little league and tennis; long hair and colorful clothing; fathers in hospital delivery rooms, in the kitchen, and changing babies' diapers; and mothers working outside the home, repairing the car, and balancing the monthly bank statements.

How you feel about the activities of your own young children, what you say to them about their "male" and "female" involvements, and what example you set depend on how you were raised and how much you recognize the changes taking place all around us. When many of us were young, boys were boys and parents usually felt that they had to be tough, protective, and sports-minded…and girls were expected to be feminine and dependent. Some of those expectations still exist, of course. Every society has certain male and female roles related to work and family, but the line between them is less clear these days. Do you really think that all men are better with tools and have to "take it" without tears even when it hurts? Do only women change their minds and become poor automobile drivers?

Male and female behavior begins in early childhood. It depends on what parents and teachers of young children consider important. In addition, children's attitudes often result from parents' responses to children's behavior. For example, a little boy who helps his father fix a faucet and receives a smile as a "thank you" begins to get the idea that approval comes from such activities. And the little girl who helps mother make a cake and receives a hug in return may think that it pays off to do "female" things.

Young children copy their parents without even knowing they do. Watch how your children walk, eat, and act toward others, and you'll see a little (or a lot) of yourself. Listen to them talk to other children, and you'll quickly see how much you influence their behavior by your example.

Here are some factors related to the attitudes of boys and girls toward the sex that they are:

- A father can be gentle and not necessarily a "sports nut," and still provide a strong example for a boy to follow. More important is the fact that he makes decisions, carries family responsibilities, and is admired for the many things he does.
- A mother can work outside the home and share the family burdens, and also show her young daughter the satisfaction she derives from being a woman.
- Parents are often attracted to their own youngsters of the opposite sex. For example, it isn't unusual for the feminine little girl to be difficult all day (with her mother) and a complete pleasure in the evening (with her father).
- Just because you are a "single parent family" doesn't mean your son or daughter will necessarily lose a great deal because the "proper" model isn't there.
- Children's attitudes toward their own sex and body and toward the opposite sex begin early. You can help form them in a healthy way.
- Young children sometimes compete for the affection of the opposite parent—boys against fathers, girls against mothers. It is usually a losing battle and doesn't last long.

It's not fair to young children to try forcing them to be only hard or callous without affection or tenderness (boys) or to assist and watch without being involved (girls). The example we set and what we expect can help children grow up to realize that both sexes are important, many interests that one has can also belong to the other, and to be "the man of the family" or "the woman of the house" may not really differ much in connection with the many things both do and enjoy.

The Two-Year-Old— Really Terrible?

Are two-year-olds a terror to live with? An old educational film presented them that way, and it wasn't all wrong. It wasn't entirely correct either.

You may often ask whether two-year-olds really have to keep getting out of bed, wetting themselves, whining, and speaking so they are hard to understand. But they can be enjoyable, too—when they laugh at the whole funny world as they bend over and look at it upside down between their legs, or imitate how you wash your hands, brush your teeth, shave, throw a ball, whistle, or talk on the telephone.

They want to feed themselves (and it may be a mess), set the table (all wrong), dry the dishes (and drop them). They listen to you, but don't hear all you say, and watch you, maybe more than you know. But that's how they learn. You are their main teacher.

You may want to put them into a preschool because they are big or mature enough, or because you have to go to work. It may be exactly the right thing to do *if* you check it out thoroughly—people, program, facilities, equipment, and materials.

It is important for you to know what two-year-olds are like so that you don't expect too much or too little. But you have to use these age guidelines carefully. A child may skip whole stages of speech, walking or running, climbing, and jumping, and still be "normal." Parents sometimes worry needlessly if their child doesn't develop exactly like others they see in the playground or at a preschool. So with that warning in mind, let's look at what many two-year-olds are like during this stage when they always seem to be in motion, so often say "No," and have more energy than both their parents together.

Language Development
- Uses a lot of sounds clearly and correctly (like m, b, and p) but not others (like r, l, s, and f)
- Says sentences that may include three or four words
- Asks for things at the table by their correct names
- Understands a lot more than he can say
- Likes to point to and name objects in a picture book

Personal or Social Development
- Plays alone or next to (but not necessarily *with*) someone else; may not like to share toys
- Is shy or cautious with strangers
- Likes to receive praise; needs quick success
- Laughs, cries, or even squeals with happiness easily
- Enjoys imitating what you do

Motor Development
- Runs without falling (but not always!)
- Walks up and down stairs, and enjoys it
- Throws a ball overhand, and likes to kick it
- Claps hands...opens doors
- Turns pages in a book, one at a time
- Enjoys "rough and tumble" play
- Builds a tower of six or seven blocks
- Scribbles (but it doesn't make much sense)
- Holds a cup or glass, and uses a spoon well
- Helps dress and undress
- Enjoys playing with water (bathtime is fun)
- And...may push, kick, bite, pinch, or poke fingers into holes

Your two-year-old may do more or less than all of that or speak more or less clearly, and still be right on target for her age. A skilled preschool teacher who has observed many children can be objective in evaluating your youngster's abilities and needs and suggest the best kind of toys, equipment, and family activities.

Two-year-olds may be difficult to live with, but they are often fun, too, if you can only relax a bit. To be with them all day every day is frequently difficult. That's an understatement...it may drive you up a wall!

The Three-Year-Old—
Really Trusting?

An educational film some years ago referred to three-year-old children as "trusting." Perhaps that word was used in contrast with "terrible" (as applied to two-year-olds). Maybe it indicated that if parents can survive the younger age, a three-year-old will be easier to live with. But not always. The child may have a big pile of worries...about dogs, people who look "odd," death or separation from parents, getting hurt, being "made differently" from a sister (or brother), or darkness, thunder, or lightning. A tired or tense parent may have trouble handling these concerns.

Three-year-olds are often less difficult to be with than they were a year earlier. They frequently like to hear stories over and over again (and that can be tiresome for some parents), have fun with make-believe playmates and animals, and play alone for longer periods. They may begin to play and share with others, too. And because they are often eager to please you, they may be easier to spend time with. Three-year-olds are usually ready for a preschool that is well-planned and professionally operated.

What are three-year-olds really like? The list below—plus living with one—will help you find out. But, remember, they are all different... develop differently...act differently...and can still be "normal."

Language Development
- Knows a few rhymes
- Likes nonsense sounds; giggles about them
- May seem to "stutter" because ideas are bigger than the child's vocabulary (but don't use that label)
- Uses five- or six-word sentences
- May name three or more objects in a picture

- Knows one color or more
- Answers questions (and can ask plenty of them!)

Personal or Social Development
- Begins to play with others; likes company
- Understands taking turns
- Dresses self, but may need supervision
- Shows an interest in more and more things outside self
- Takes care of most toilet needs
- Understands hazards (the street, automobiles, swimming pools, stoves); begins to learn "right" from "wrong"
- May need a nap-time rest, but not necessarily sleep
- Notices sex differences (answer questions simply and honestly)

Motor Development
- Pedals a tricycle
- Can unbutton one or two buttons
- Pours from a pitcher (sometimes without spilling)
- Alternates feet going upstairs
- Stands on one foot for a second or more
- Runs and jumps easily; likes to try almost anything
- Feeds self rather neatly
- Puts together puzzles, maybe up to 6 or 8 pieces
- Scribbles more clearly than last year

A well-experienced preschool teacher can tell you whether your three-year-old is within the "normal" range and what toys, materials, and equipment can help meet your child's needs. This age is often the start of better days ahead, help in cleaning up the kitchen or bedroom, for example. But don't expect too much. After all, a three-year-old is still pretty small and immature.

The Four-Year-Old— Frustrating?

"No"…" I won't"…bossiness…lying without meaning to…that may all be part of your four-year-old's days. The four-year-old is not always a joy to live with. Now the four-year-old talks even more and may listen better than last year, and takes care of meal and toilet needs more carefully. "How?" and "Why?" are frequent questions, and if you have the time and patience, the questions can be fun to answer. A good preschool may help you live through each day more easily, whether you are a working parent or not. It can provide friends, activities, toys, and equipment that even the best home cannot offer.

Like all children (and some adults), four-year-olds are not the same. Their personalities, interests, and language skills differ a great deal and yet they may be within the "normal" range. Those who work with groups of children every day can be more objective in observing whether your youngster is within that level. However, a checklist can help you if you don't use it too strictly. Here is one for you to try out—but carefully.

Language Development
- Talks a lot…may go on and on with one topic…asks questions again and again and again
- Likes puppets; imitates adults and animals
- Knows three or four colors; counts fingers, or higher numbers
- Puts silly words together, and laughs at them

Personal or Social Development
- "Plays house" and with dolls…boys do, too
- Has imaginary playmates and likes to pretend in play (cowboys/cowgirls and firefighters, for example)

- Likes to play with sand, water, mud, paint, crayons, and chalk (sometimes easier to live with in a preschool setting than at home!)
- Plays with other children better than a year or two ago, but argues with them, too; may be boastful and bossy
- Makes up stories about friends and himself or herself; doesn't think of them as "lies"; truth and fiction get all mixed up together
- Brushes teeth, washes face, and dresses and undresses with little or no supervision

Motor Development
- Runs, climbs, and hops easily
- Stands on one foot for two to five seconds
- Can button clothes and perhaps lace shoes
- Holds pencils, crayons, and paint brushes as adults do
- Can walk heel-to-toe for three, four or more steps with one foot close to the front of the other one
- Shows more skill in cutting, throwing, and jumping

The life of the four-year-old gets bigger and bigger—both in what the children do and say. You can help expand it through a costume box, puppets, a chalkboard, and other inexpensive materials and toys. Equipment to ride, climb on, push, and pull generally cost more. That's where a sound preschool or neighborhood or park playground can come in handy. The "frustrating" four-year-old needs your love and patience most of all. Next come other adults, outside, with whom you can share the burden. It may be good for your mental health to do so once in a while!

The Five-Year-Old— Fascinating?

The days of babyhood are fading away. Formal school years lie ahead. An old educational film referred to this in-between time as "fascinating," and it often is. However, no stage of child growth and development runs smoothly. There are always adjustments, tears, and noise, as well as laughter and happiness. Even though five-year-olds are often easier to live with than younger children, they need your interest and attention, and maybe even more of your time. They have a lot to say and ask about, and more fears, questions, and conflicts related to their friends, brothers and sisters, and you. It is a big, mystifying, wonderful world, and they need your help in figuring it out.

They may listen to you more than they did earlier, but every good, honest answer may bring another question. Usually they really want to "know something," but sometimes it's all just to hear themselves talk or to fill silence with some words, any words.

Five-year-olds differ from each other, as they did when they were two, three, and four. A checklist like the one that follows may help you see whether your child is in the "normal" range. A child may, of course, not check out on all the items and still be "normal."

Language Development
- Identifies nickels, dimes, and pennies by name
- Counts to ten, maybe higher; likes to play counting and alphabet games
- Looks at pictures, and comments on people, colors, and other factors not noticed before
- Begins to understand "time" words related to the clock and calendar, birthdays, and holidays

- Tells stories, makes up some, and exchanges ideas in detail with play-mates
- May actually be able to read...or sometimes merely pretends
- Watches a television show all the way through and can discuss it
- Still asks "Why?" questions, so your answers are wanted (even though they are not always listened to!)

Personal or Social Development
- Plays well in groups, with little supervision...two are usually fine—three may be argumentative
- Dresses self quite well
- Finishes a project started
- Does a good job in washing self, but may still need reminding
- "Plays house" and with dolls, but these days are numbered for boys

Motor Development
- Can handle simple tools and equipment safely
- Shows definite right- or left-handedness
- Can use all table implements, even a knife
- Balances on one foot for up to eight or ten seconds
- Skips, using each foot alternately
- May be able to tie a knot
- Can copy a square, print a few letters and draw a person with several parts you can recognize

Your five-year-old is nearing the end of the most important developmental years of his or her life. If the child has had a family life where each person is important, where there is at least some time for talking and listening, where smiles, touching and hugging are part of each day, then your five-year-old is no doubt ready for the big adventures that lie ahead.

The Large Muscles of Little Children

Before a child goes to school, she has to learn many important things. Among the most important are how her body works and how to use her arms and legs. Although they all come together kind of naturally, you can help prepare for the large and small muscle development everyone needs. Teachers and others talk about "gross motor" (large muscle) and "fine motor" (small muscle) activities. With a little time and some inexpensive equipment, you can help your young child make good use of the controls and strengths important now and later. The child will, of course, run, jump, climb, hop, and skip without your involvement, but you may not be aware of the large number of skills you can help add.

How much equipment and material is available in the preschool your child attends, or in your own yard or neighborhood playground or park? (No child needs all of it. All children can learn by using much of it, however.) And is it all *safe* and *sturdy*? It'll be taking a lot of punishment.

Equipment and materials: stairs, skates, barrel, wheelbarrow, balls (all sizes), seesaw, boxes and blocks, boards (2 x 4s and flat ones), slide and bars, swings and gym set, ladder (rope and wall), trains, trucks and cars, shovel and broom, bean bags and hoops, tricycle, and wagon.

No two children (even in the same family) mature at the same rate or necessarily like the same playthings. Your child may enjoy some toys; another child might prefer others. Yours may be ready for some at three; others are ready earlier or later. Here are a few sample activities that experts say preschool children can often do at different ages. Remember, your youngster may be slower or faster and still be completely "normal."

2 to 3 years old
- Runs without falling
- Opens doors; turns door knobs
- Walks up and down stairs
- Jumps with both feet
- Builds small block tower
- Stands on tiptoes
- Tries to stand on one foot

3 to 4 years old
- Rides a tricycle
- Kicks a ball
- Jumps from bottom step
- Throws ball overhand
- Walks on a circle without stepping off
- Changes feet going upstairs or on a board (or "balance beam")
- Stands and hops on one foot

4 to 5 years old
- Jumps while running or standing still
- Stops, starts, and turns corners quickly
- Changes feet going downstairs
- Builds tall block tower
- Balances well on toes
- Hops on one foot
- Walks heel to toe
- Climbs ladders and trees

One kind of "equipment" that almost any child can have is an old automobile tire. What the child does with it may surprise you…walking on the rim, jumping in and out, and putting feet on the tire with hands on the floor. With a few tries, children often jump from inside one to another, and run forward and backward in designs and patterns that are fun for them.

Although a young child needs independence in developing muscular coordination, balance and strength, parents and teachers can be very helpful. *Showing how, doing with, holding hands*, and *praising effort and success can all pay off*. Start with what the child can do and lead into new activities. Does this all sound like a tough job for parents? It certainly doesn't have to be, if you bring at least a little time and patience to it. You may be surprised—you might even enjoy it. One thing is very sure—your young child certainly will.

Day Care and Preschools

The Early Years—
Don't Waste Them

The young child needs friends his age and size with whom he can communicate and cooperate. He needs recognition and social acceptance for his abilities, character and personality. The family alone, as precious and good as it is, cannot meet all of these needs.—Dr. Frances Horwich ("Miss Frances," Ding Dong School)

Authorities in this field know that an early childhood program can pay off—if it is prepared especially for young children and operated by competent persons who understand them, know how they develop, and work closely with their parents.

Those who believe in the value of preschools feel that a well-planned early experience in such settings can pay rich dividends. Both the child and his or her parents will benefit from it. Respectable researchers say it all in different ways. It is sometimes difficult to cut through their big words, but their ideas are very clear as they write about young children who receive this early enrichment.

- *...one might expect the environment to have its greatest impact during the first years of life.*
- *...gains in 'intelligence,' as well as...language growth.*
- *...durable effects on IQ scores and reading level...*
- *...more socially accepted...*
- *...higher...on measures of academic achievement, IQ, and social-emotional development...general information scores and mathematics achievement...*
- *...cope more effectively with the demands of school...*

One skilled researcher in the field said:

...No thinking persons (should) ignore the importance of the first few years of life...I (can) continue to cite data...until you could not possibly refuse to conclude that early childhood enrichment produces impressive gains in the intellectual functioning of young children...At this stage in the history of early childhood education, most of us inside the field are over the hurdle of 'does early childhood education produce positive effects.'

Yes, they answer emphatically, as one did after reviewing 227 studies in this area. They found less tension and better "social interaction scores" among those with day care experience even in infancy, and "no evidence that infant day care and the separation from mother leads to emotional insecurity."

All of these ideas relate to a widely quoted statement about the importance of the early years (Dr. Benjamin S. Bloom, University of Chicago). He wrote: "...in terms of intelligence...about 50% of the development takes place between conception and age 4, about 30% between ages 4 and 8 and about 20% between ages 8 and 17...*as much of the development takes place in the first 4 years of life as in the next 13 years.*" (My emphasis).

To be fair, it must be stated that a few serious objections have been raised to early childhood programs. It is wrong to take the child from his or her family, they say. Of course it is. No well-planned preschools "take away" children from their families. Their goal is to *add* to a young child's experiences and home environment during these vital early years.

The objectors sometimes talk about the dangers to attitudes, relationships, and children's eyes of "early schooling," but this early enrichment is not formal "schooling." The reading to, playing with, number games, music, art, dance, and all the rest are related and sometimes preparation for, but not part of, such "schooling." Young children should not sit at desks, read, and study. Most of them are not ready to do so. No competent preschool educator says they should.

Some of those who oppose these programs cite the danger of "depriving children of warmth and security." Of course, it is possible, but a sound early childhood program provides both in abundance. The teachers' skills and personalities add to what a child can receive from a warm and secure family and home. Children can profit from the richness of an expanded environment. Researchers, preschool teachers, and thoughtful parents all know this. The pay-off is in the words and smiles of little boys and girls. Watch them, listen to them, and you will get part of the answer to this question: Is an early childhood program worthwhile?

You can Select a Preschool

You go to work every day…there are no other children around… she talks poorly, won't sit still, reads the TV commercials, or wants to go to school. Perhaps most of these statements are true. Your youngster is two, three, or four, and you think it's time to look for a preschool (or nursery school or day care center). How do you find one that will be good for your child and that is worth the child's time and your money?

You can start by checking on the items below. If a preschool won't let you visit to find out about its staff and activities, that's your first warning signal. This checklist can help you select a good place for your young child, or make you feel comfortable about the one your youngster now attends.

- *General atmosphere.* Is it a happy place? Do the children seem to enjoy themselves? Is there music? Is children's art on the walls? Are there singing, dancing, and smiling little and big people?
- *Good teachers.* Do you like the way teachers look and act with the children and toward you? Are they prepared for their work, either college courses or on-the-job training, or both? Do they seem well-adjusted, warm but firm, and flexible? Is there enough professional personnel for the number of children?
- *Program.* Is there a planned program that you can see on paper and in action?
- *Equipment and materials.* Are they the kind which young children enjoy and from which they can learn? Are some of them creative and exciting? Are they safe?
- *Cost.* Is the price right for you? (You often get what you pay for!)
- *Records.* Do teachers keep records on each child and point out possible learning and adjustment problems? Do they seem to know each child

well enough to do that? (Early identification of learning, physical, mental, speech, and emotional difficulties is very important.)

- *Parent conferences.* Are teachers willing to share information about your child with you? Do they do so in words you can understand and in enough detail that you can act on what they tell you? Do they welcome your questions and comments?
- *Child setting.* Are the tables, chairs, steps, clothes hooks, shelves, and bathrooms made for little children?
- *Space.* Is there enough indoor and outdoor space for quiet and active play and work? Is there an "isolation room" for a sick child?
- *Safety, cleanliness, and health.* Do they have fire protection, liability insurance, good lighting, adequate ventilation, and clean water and toilet facilities? Are there daily rest times, health inspections, and well-prepared meals?
- *Creativity.* Do the children have many different experiences each day and frequent chances to talk and listen to other youngsters and adults —or do they all do the same thing at the same time, day after day after day?
- *Readiness for later schooling.* Do they help your child get ready to read, understand and use numbers, and develop physically with enjoyable activities rather than rigid lessons for which the child is still too little or immature?
- *Social adjustment.* Can you see these in operation: Sharing, standing up for their rights, time to be alone as well as time in groups. Do teachers calmly, fairly, firmly help children understand that they can't always have their own way?
- *Attitudes.* Does there seem to be a good attitude toward children of other races and religions, and toward their own bodies and bodily functions?
- *Follow-through and respect.* Are the children helped to finish tasks and be careful of what belongs to others?

Good private and public preschools will "pass" most of these items. Poor ones will not—and your child needs your protection from them. What children do and learn during these early years will determine their later health, attitudes toward school, and the kind of people they will grow up to be. Their future happiness is often the result of how well we help them start out. These 15 items are one way to put a little child on the right track.

Leaving Your Child at Preschool— Tears, Screams, or What?

You want your young child to enjoy the preschool experience, to look forward to being there, and to like the children, teacher, learning, and play. But sometimes parents are worried, maybe even feel a little guilty (especially if they are working mothers or single parents), and wonder whether they are doing the right thing. A little reading and checking ahead of time can pay off—and then you'll be ready for this three-pronged approach.

Before the child goes. Try to remember that this is a big unknown for your youngster. Even adults are often a little fearful of what lies ahead in a new experience, so we shouldn't be surprised if little children are. It is generally helpful to talk about the preschool in a pleasant, matter-of-fact way in advance. You might mention toys, games, music, art, dance, or any activities that you know your child enjoys which are available in good preschools. There will also be children to play with and nice teachers to learn from. Your emphasis on preschool as a happy place is very important, but you'll get the point across best if you really feel it is.

You may want to visit the preschool alone before you take your youngster there. Among the things you will want to find out is *what will happen on your child's first day*; specifics are vital so you can then share them with your youngster.

An important tour (or more than one). Plan ahead so that the visit with your child is when there is action—inside or playground activities or snack time, not a nap period. Introduce your youngster to the adults there, and let him or her see every part where children are, including bathrooms and lunch areas. If your child wants to try out some of the toys or play equipment or join a group, that's fine—and if their personnel objects, you might want to seek another preschool. It is also a good time for questions from both of you about the people, program, and facilities.

The first day. Sure, you may be concerned, but not much if you've checked it out, visited alone and together, received good answers, can afford what it costs, and have an eager young child by the hand. Then it'll be easier to put on that important "happy face."

Leaving your child with the right person, one whom you both met earlier, a single hug and kiss, a promise (that you must keep) to return later—and that's about it. Don't turn around or look back even if you hear a familiar cry or sob; it will probably be over as soon as you leave anyway. A skillful teacher (the only kind to whom you should loan your "treasure") will smoothly involve your child in activities that can change tears to happy involvement. A rapid adjustment can come through introduction to a group, a cooperative child partner, a chance to assist with routine activities (helping serve juice or taking out or putting away toys) and to participate or just watch, and using the child's name often. A few hours later you might telephone to see how things are going. That call can accomplish two purposes: Show that you are a parent who will keep in contact with them and put your mind at ease.

When you pick up your youngster, talk about the enjoyable things he did, played with, and learned. Try not to dwell on negative events; listen to everything, but concentrate on positive items. Let this be your pattern every day. If there are problems, you might ask yourself, "Have I talked about the preschool in a pleasant way? Do I leave my child each day without hesitation, not turning back, showing that I feel it's a good spot? Is it an enjoyable place?" This all adds up to one of the most significant events in a child's growing up and in our cutting "the silver cord." Careful planning will assure a happy and successful experience for both of you.

It's a Different Kind of School

Why is your child in a preschool program? Perhaps you have a job—or there are no other youngsters where you live—or it'll be good for him—or your friends' kids are in one. What do you really want your child to get out of it?

Your expectations make sense to you, even though you probably didn't have this opportunity when you were young. In those days people didn't realize how much of a child's intelligence is developed by age five.

A healthy early childhood program isn't just a baby-sitting service—nor is it like the orderly classroom of your first school experience. When you visit, you can expect to see many activities happening at one time. Even though it may sometimes seem noisy and confused, there is a plan at work. It is based on clear-cut objectives, like these:

Learning about self. The child is finding out that he can plan something and follow through, whether it's connected with block building, painting, cutting and pasting, or taking care of himself at meals or in the bathroom. He is learning that he can understand books, listen to records, set the table, and help select which visit to make or seeds to plant. He knows that he is getting bigger and stronger. He begins to see that he can get along with other children and is finding out that he has changing likes and dislikes in food, toys, and games.

Getting ready for reading. A child really begins to learn to read in infancy, when she starts to differentiate between bright red and pale pink, dull pablum and a delicious apricot flavor, her mother and everyone else. Such early differences are sharpened and refined during the two-to-five years. She hears stories, acts them out, and talks about them. She gets ready to read by saying and understanding more words, going more places, and seeing more things. The increasing ability to express herself and to listen to what you say

relates directly to how well she will soon interpret pages in a book.
Developing the senses. Although most of what we all have learned came
through our eyes, we missed a lot. The other senses—hearing, touch, taste,
and smell—can stimulate a child to learn a great deal about himself and the
world around him. When are shapes the same or different—what do words
like "right," "left," "up," "down," "in," "out," and "around" mean—how can the
textures of burlap, velvet, and sandpaper be described? All these help a child
grow up when they are talked about with a teacher who listens, who makes a
youngster feel important, and who encourages conversation.

Contributing to physical development. Most of us can't afford smooth slides,
safe swings, bars, pulleys, balance beams, or other creative equipment that
contribute toward the development of large muscles. Nor do we have the time
and patience to encourage small muscle development through matching,
measuring, collecting, putting puzzles together, stringing beads, and building
with small blocks, sticks, and stones. But these child settings do all that and
much more.

   That's only the beginning of what you'll see in many well-operated day
care/child care/nursery schools/preschools. They teach numbers through
enjoyable counting games, getting your youngster ready for arithmetic. They
help the child understand that she can't always have her own way, and that
tantrums, grabbing and screaming don't pay off. The teachers still accept and
love her, but they show that they don't necessarily like what she does,
through their calm, fair, firm handling rather than through adult anger.
They teach safety with toys, in a tree, and on the street, and how to get along
peacefully with others, listen quietly, and express ideas so that others understand. These preschools carry quite a load that helps pave the way toward
better learning at school and easier living at home.

The P/P/P
(Parent-Preschool Partnership)

When you send your child off to a nursery school, preschool, or child care center, do you ever have a guilty feeling? Many parents do, whether their reason for enrolling the child is so they can go to work or just to have some free time.

A good way to look at the situation is as a partnership in which you and the center are both involved for the youngster's benefit. No matter how long your child is there each day, you remain as the "senior partner" with the major responsibility for guiding and shaping her into the kind of person you want her to be. However, their personnel can be very helpful if the two-way communication between home and school is kept open. Here are three of the most important areas in which it can be put to work:

Getting along with other children. The preschool can tell you who his best friends are, which toys he enjoys sharing with others and which he likes to play with alone, and concerns they have about his being bossy or shy and what they are trying to do about it. You can let them know what difficulties you have in arranging for him to be with other youngsters (because of your work schedule, where you live, or other reasons), the kinds of social or solitary play situations, toys and equipment available to him at home and in your neighborhood, and how he acts with children when you observe him. You and they can compare how the child performs at home and in school. Sharing information can help both of you follow up on what the other is doing.

Developing language skills. From the day care/preschool you can find out how your child's vocabulary and speech patterns compare with those of other children her age. They can fill you in on what they are doing to develop them, through telling and acting out stories and talking about plans for the painting, music, counting, meal, playground, and other activities scheduled in sound child centers. At home you can supplement their work by reading to her, talking about her day's events, and mainly doing what comes so hard to most adults—listening to what she has to say. If they tell you about her specific language and speech strengths and weaknesses (and what they are doing to capitalize on or eliminate them), their approach will give you an idea of what you can do in the time you have her at home. And when you tell them you are worried about how she pronounces certain words ("yady" for "lady," for example), they can indicate whether that's normal for her age or really a problem.

Accepting responsibilities. Well-organized preschools don't just talk about helping youngsters become more responsible. They move that objective into action as the child puts toys away, gets into and out of clothing, cleans up the watercoloring area, arranges the table for lunch, helps plan the little garden or window box plants, and feeds the goldfish, mice, rabbits, or gerbils. They can supervise such activities, but they can't—and shouldn't—have the sole responsibility for helping him grow up.

The "senior partner" has to follow through with the toys, dressing, clean up, table setting, planning, and animals (if there are any) at home. The teacher and her aides can tell you what to expect (a two-year-old putting away one toy is something to be pleased with, for instance) and what they are working on at the preschool to help your child accept responsibilities appropriate to his age and development. You can share any particular skills you'd also like them to emphasize.

Teachers don't have your youngster for the whole day, evening, and weekends, and neither do you. If you aren't aware of what play and work activities they are involved in and they don't know what needs and concerns you feel, your child may not get the most from what can be a rich experience. This parent-preschool partnership can provide a solid foundation for later school success and home adjustment. Through it you will obtain a clear picture of what your youngster can do now and where the child's potential abilities and problems lie.

Kindergarten Comes Next

Is your young child going to kindergarten next fall? What can you do to help him or her get ready? All kindergartens are, of course, not the same. There are three main types:

- One is like other grades in some schools, where the teachers teach reading, arithmetic, science, and all the rest, and want order and quiet.
- Another kind is much less "school-like." The children may not learn very much, but they might have a good time playing.
- Most are somewhere between those two. Work and play melt together in days filled with activities.

A good kindergarten is a busy, happy place. It is probably a lot different today than it was when you were five years old. There are books and animals. Children plan and work, alone and with others. They make and read charts of colors, numbers, weather, and room helpers. They use clocks and calendars. They learn safety with tools and equipment, and health habits in washing hands, using the toilet, and sometimes eating meals. They learn to share ideas, finish tasks, listen, and follow directions. They get ready to read and use numbers.

Not all kindergarten teachers expect the same things of the children who come to them. It is, of course, fine if your preschool child can tell time, knows the days of the week and months of the year (in order), and can make change and knows the names of coins. But all of that isn't always expected. There is time to learn such skills, plus the beginnings of reading as well as a home address and telephone number and how to write them.

A child who likes to be the center of attention and wants his or her own way may have a hard time adjusting to school. The one who is timid and says, "I can't," needs your help and patience to get over such feelings. The child who cries because her fancy dress or his new shirt or tie gets a little crushed or dirty needs to have you know how children should dress for their school day (in bright, durable, easily laundered clothing).

You can also do many other things to help your youngster prepare for kindergarten. Some of the main ones are enough sleep (10-12 hours each night), balanced meals, a medical checkup and necessary shots, how to use a drinking fountain, toilet away from home, and handkerchief (or tissues) correctly, and how to cross streets. The dangers of wooden swings and throwing things are among the safety factors your child should know. The example you set for good health and safety is very important.

Go with the child to visit the school and its playground. Talk about it as a happy place. Remember that it probably will seem very large, crowded, and noisy to the child. Expect him to be a little worried—but help him see it as a place of excitement and fun. Keep in mind that work is enjoyable for most young children, and school will probably be, too. Make an appointment to visit the kindergarten with your child so that you both can find out about its program. What did you each see there? Talk to him about it. Let the child tell you what he liked and what he may have wondered about.

The activities you can provide will help make the move from home and preschool to kindergarten more smooth. Read to him, let him tell or finish stories and button and zip himself up, visit the library with him, work out the household tasks he can do with dishes, clothes, putting toys away, caring for animals, and watering plants.

Don't worry if he has been going to a fine preschool, day care center, or nursery school and you think the regular school will not be as good. No matter his age, your plan should be to get the best education possible at all times. With kindergarten coming up soon, you can help most by finding out and letting the child find out what it will be like and providing experiences and information that will make this new learning situation comfortable and happy.

Teach Your Child Well

Learning is More
than Eyes and Ears

"Eat your food...go to sleep...stop that...come here..." Young children learn early to listen to what you say. "Did you see...look at that...watch me..."

They also know that it is fun to see new toys, TV cartoons, colorful books, and slides and swings. But *learning is more than hearing and seeing,* even though most of the abilities of little children to talk, explore, climb, and share come directly through the sights and sounds all around them. However, parents too often depend on just the eyes and ears. Good preschool teachers know how much a child can learn and grow through *all* the senses. They sometimes use fancy words to describe the total pattern through which young children develop, including these:

Sensory development. A young child can *feel* the difference between hot and cold, *see* the difference between black and white, *taste* the difference between salt and sugar, *hear* the difference between a fire engine siren and a bird's song, and *smell* the difference between an onion and a flower. You can talk with your young child about these and many other differences all around us when you have dinner, go for a walk or ride, or watch television together.

Language development. During the preschool years *you can use words in sentences that a little child uses by themselves.* "Shoe" can become "let's tie your shoe," "eat" can change to "yes, it's time to eat lunch," and "nap" can move into "you're now ready to have your nap, to rest for awhile."

Perceptual or concept development. Children see and hear differences before they fully understand them. When a child knows and can explain (even in simple terms) how or why something does or doesn't look, taste, smell, feel, or sound like something else, the child has more understanding. *Your "how" and "why" questions can help the youngster figure out reasons for the differences.*

Hands, eyes, ears, mouths, and noses are tools for learning. Sometimes it is difficult for parents to live comfortably with that thought. A finger in a light socket, peas pushed into little ears, a tongue eagerly tasting a dirty stone or a furry puppy—these are the kinds of exploration that test the mental health of even calm parents. They are the types of activities that may call for "preventive discipline" (removing the temptation or problem in advance) rather than the "don't… stop hitting" routine that may seem to be necessary at the moment.

Safety does come first, of course, but children can't and shouldn't be deprived of the important opportunity to find out more about this exciting, new world of theirs. And they have to use all of their senses to do so. The big differences between the sound of a loud bell and a whisper, the sight of an elephant and a fly, or the smell and taste of vinegar and chocolate are just the beginning.

As parents we can help our youngster's preschool teachers refine the use of their senses. Violet and purple, cooked and raw cabbage, this small flower and leaf and that one, this coarse sandpaper and that fine variety—the differences and similarities that surround us are easy to identify and fun to point out and talk about.

Learning that takes place later depends on these early experiences. For example, reading relates to what children hear and see, and the words they understand and use in the first years. The basis for reading actually begins in infancy when the first differences are noticed (this dull baby food against that apricot-flavored type, or this big red ball against that little tan one) and continues during the preschool years, until this word ("cat") is understood as different from that one ("mat" or "pat" or "bat" or "rat").

Using all the senses can help each child do well in later schooling and in understanding and appreciating this beautiful world in which we live. Practice in using them should begin very early in our homes through the talking, listening, stories, and time so difficult for working (and *all*) parents to share with their young children.

Consistency—A Parent's Must

The most important word in marriage is probably "compatibility." The most important word in raising children may be "consistency." Well, perhaps it isn't quite as significant as "health" and a few others that might occur to you, but in most families it deserves to be near the top. Without it, children often play one parent against the other, might be confused by what they are told to do, and perhaps will not receive the stable start that helps them become healthy, well-adjusted adults.

Among the areas of parent-child relationships in which consistency is most necessary are *discipline, behavior, diet and nutrition, scheduling,* and *mother/father agreement.*

Discipline. You shouldn't punish a child one day for being sloppy with water, mud, crayons, or paints and compliment her the next day in the same kind of mess for being so "artistic." A young child should know ahead of time your rules related to coming when she is called…going to a neighbor's house or leaving a preschool without permission…playing dangerously in a car, on the street, or with a strange dog.

Because young children are so eager to please their parents, they usually respond well when you tell them what a good job they did, whether it is with the dishes, setting the table, or brushing their teeth. Your guidance is most effective if your children always know what you expect of them.

Behavior. Children's behavior can be changed, but to alter it, your consistency is essential. Keep a record of behaviors you want to improve, and use a smile, hug, or other pleasant recognition when they are reached. Such warm reactions may accomplish more than repeated scolding or nagging.

Your goal should be to establish habits that make living with young children more rewarding and easier, whether it means putting toys away, finishing a meal, getting ready for bed, or establishing good bathroom performance. Each time a child tends toward the goal you seek, your approval must be there, quickly and honestly.

Diet and nutrition. Soft drinks and candy are either all right for children, or they are not. It can't be a "sometimes" thing. Your attitude toward them should be the same, no matter what day it is or how you feel—and for all of your children, regardless of their age. It isn't fair for either the older ones or you to set the example of eating junk foods or meals at odd hours, and expect the preschool child not to notice and want to share the freedom and flexibility.

Scheduling. Whenever a young child's daily schedule changes, there should be a reason that the child can understand. "Later dinner?...There is that wonderful TV show I want to watch with you." "Stay up a little longer?...Let's finish reading this book together." "Miss preschool today?... I think you have a little temperature." Little children want each day to have a pattern. However, life for all of us isn't that orderly, so helping children adapt to revised schedules should begin early—as long as it has meaning for them.

Parental agreement. Parents do not always agree on discipline, behavior, foods, schedules, and budgeting related to their children. (They obviously don't always agree when factors like these pertain to themselves either!) As difficult as it sometimes is, parents should try to present a "united front" to their children. Admitting errors of judgment ("Mother was right to let you stay up a little longer...I'm sorry I was so quick in saying you couldn't.") is a sign of parental strength, not weakness.

If young children are to know where they stand in the family and at their preschool, the adults around them must work toward a daily pattern where discipline, meals, and other factors important to their children have a dependable order. In this undependable world of ours it is difficult to provide that orderliness. Sometimes the pressure of our jobs, arguments with our husbands or wives, or health problems interfere, but the goal is clear: *To be as consistent as we possibly can toward our preschool children in what we say and do.*

Discipline and Punishment—
Where do You Stand?

He took the hose and pumped water into the gas tank of your new car...ran into the street and was almost hit...tried to hide a key in the electrical wall plug...pulled up all the violets you just planted...let the bird out of the cage, cut his friend's hair (and his friend cut his), ran away.

What do you do about situations like these? Which side are you on: 1) A hard walloping, regardless of the offense, is the best and only appropriate punishment; 2) There is never a reason to hit a young child; 3) Other kinds of punishment are often more effective?

Parents usually punish a child to prevent danger to him or destruction of something. Sometimes it's just to release their own tensions. A sound approach to discipline should include more than stopping a youngster from doing what you don't want her to do. Severe punishment given in anger may teach a child something you don't intend—that temper tantrums and hitting are acceptable behavior, as long as an adult hands it out.

The purpose of discipline is to help a child learn to behave in a desirable, safe way, and to respect the property and feelings of others. It directs him toward what he can do, where he can ride his bike, dig holes, and pound pots and pans, rather than where he can't. Children generally want to please their parents. They are seldom "bad" deliberately. You can help them do the "right" thing if you expect it, and if you tell them how well they put their things away, get ready for bed, and brush their teeth. Your smiles, approval, and love are very important. Here are ten common-sense guidelines to discipline. Perhaps they can help prevent problems and useless punishment with your own preschool child.

- Discipline and punishment are not the same thing. A well-disciplined child may seldom have to be punished. Learning right from wrong can frequently come through your patient explanations, your own carefulness (crossing streets, using tools, and shutting car doors, for example), and temporarily depriving him of something he wants.
- Young children need limits and controls. They can't handle total freedom. But they should have the chance to create, experiment, and make simple decisions.
- Spankings and yelling may sometimes be avoided if you use "preventive discipline." Problems with valuable breakables, medicines, and hot soup can all be prevented. Besides, they aren't as much fun as washable crayons (and an acceptable place to use them), blocks that fit together, and a colorful book you can read together.
- Children usually behave better when they are busy, and not so well when they are bored or tired.
- No single set of rules or punishment fits all children. The shy, quiet child needs encouragement to open up, and parental strictness may be a mistake. For the secure, outgoing child a few rules and restrictions, carefully developed and clearly understood, may provide important guidance.
- You can confuse a young child if you offer choices when the decision should be yours. "Do you want to go to bed?" gives him a chance to say, "No!" Then you might get into the "Yes-you-will-no-I-won't" routine.
- Harsh punishment may be remembered—but not the reason for it. Endless scoldings, the silent treatment, shame, and ridicule are generally not very effective with young children. Words and looks are sometimes enough to show disapproval.
- Occasionally there are good reasons for changing the rules. More important than nap time may be what she's doing right at that moment. Respect for her interests can help avoid conflicts.
- Some of the best discipline comes in relationships with others. The child will learn that being selfish about toys and hitting friends does not pay off; they'll just play with others or go home.
- Your expectations should be realistic. We sometimes forget that it takes two to five years to learn all the rules of safety, respect for others, and self-control.

One additional factor is important. With all the pressures you face every day, perhaps you can't always be as calm as you might like to be. It is good for your children to learn early to "roll with" your moods and needs just as you try to adjust to theirs. That ability is also part of good discipline.

Changing the Behavior of Young Children—Can it be Done?

Does your preschool child do some things you don't like? Does he or she hit or bite, refuse to eat or go to sleep, or fail to put toys away? Do you want to improve things and make life more pleasant for both of you? You have two choices: Continue as you are, perhaps with nagging, screaming, and hitting of your own—or go at it with a plan, in an orderly way. The first choice may seem easier, but it's probably not very successful. The second takes longer, but it may work better.

Some behavior is changed by time. Dressing himself, eating neatly, and going to the bathroom are examples where maturity and the right models may take care of the situation. But improving other kinds of behavior needs your active help. You can start by asking: *What do I want to change? What behavior do I think needs improving?* Make a list of what he or she does that bothers you.

There are two major parts of what you can do to encourage better behavior, whether it's related to whining, striking out at others, taking things, or almost anything else that you feel is wrong. First, keep a record of what behaviors you see that you want to improve. Whenever you notice one, write it down. Do so for only one kind of behavior at first because it takes practice to keep notes of this kind. For example, how often does the child cry for what seems like no reason? If you know the reason, like being over-tired or catching a cold, then removing the cause or relieving the illness may solve the problem. Even if you know of no reason, you can start toward getting rid of the tears.

Use affection and praise to work for good behavior. If possible, pay no attention to the kind of behavior you want to stop. At first the tears or misbehavior may come even more often, but stopping them requires your sticking with a detailed procedure. When parents continue to give in, to provide the attention a child strives for when he does what we don't like, he has no reason to stop.

You'll have to notice very small changes for the better, and react to them right away. Your words, smile, hug, or just the quiet attention you give (like a shy child who makes even a slight effort to join another youngster) may be enough. Perhaps you can offer a small reward. "When you put your toys away and get ready for bed, I'll have a treat for you (milk and cookies)." Some people call this "bribery," but it isn't. Bribery is a reward for doing something wrong.

This approach is sometimes referred to as "Grandma's Law." "Do what I want and you'll get what you want"—or—"Work before play." That "play," or reward, should be something your child likes. Remember that what may be a chore for us isn't to preschool youngsters. They like to help you wash the car and set the table, and to run errands or be carried on Daddy's shoulders.

Our habit of finding fault is often a trap. Yes, a child might pick up his clothes or wash his hands this time, but it may be only temporary. You may have to nag him every time you want something done.

Many studies indicate that using certain words, expressions, and physical closeness may help us improve children's behavior. Try words like these when you see the smallest hint of improvement: "You did a good job," "Fine," "I'm so pleased," "Let's tell your Dad." Or use certain *facial expressions* more often: smiling, laughing, looking interested, nodding approval. Or *get closer* by touching, hugging, sitting on the side of the child's bed, or offering your comfortable lap.

If rewards are used to get small improvements started, they can be given less frequently as the tantrums or other troublesome activities occur less often. By the time the bad habits are over, you won't have to think about providing rewards. Researchers have worked hard in this whole field of changing children's behavior. They use words like "behavior modification," "reinforcement," "extinction," "modeling," and "shaping." Their goal is the same as ours: Increase the good behavior, reduce or eliminate the bad, and make our children's lives happier—and our own, too.

"Where did I Come From, Mama?"
(A few words about sex and the young child)

This story has been told many times. It is about a young child who asks his mother, "Where did I come from?"

Thinking this was the moment for telling her youngster all about sex—how babies are started, the differences between boys and girls, and all the rest— the mother took a deep breath and jumped right in. After a half hour of explaining (with drawings), she finally relaxed, and said, "Well, that's it, Johnny. Does that answer your question?" In a puzzled way, little Johnny replied, "No, mama. You see, my friend Billy comes from Chicago, and I just wanted to know, where did I come from?"

So, RULE #1 connected with sex and the young child is this: *Answer the question the child asks, and give only what is asked for—no more and no less.*

Some parents are surprised, and maybe even shocked, by what young children do, say, and ask about sex. If the baby discovers fingers and toes, his happy mother and father are all smiles. But if he touches his sex parts, they may think it's "bad." If the young child asks about the weather or the stars, that's great. But if he is curious about his body (or the body of the little girl next door), that may seem dangerous and something to worry about.

RULE #2, therefore, goes this way: *Curiosity about sex is just part of the young child's eagerness to learn about the whole, new, wonderful world.*

Because the beginnings of life are so mysterious and strange, the young child doesn't find out about them easily. The child picks up a little at a time, asks questions again and again, and might collect a lot of false information along the way. Facts like these may be among the ones the youngster wants:

• Only women have babies—not men or children. The stork does not bring them, either.

- A baby grows from a tiny dot to full size.
- The baby grows inside the mother, but not in her stomach where the food is.
- The baby comes out through a special opening.
- Everybody has or had both a mother and a father.
- Boys and girls are different. You can tell the child that (s)he is made exactly the way (s)he should be.

Questions related to the role of the father, menstruation, intercourse, and more involved topics generally come later.

Here is RULE #3: *Much of the young child's sex education is based on simple information, given honestly and directly. It's not wise to put it off with "I'm busy," "Wait until your father comes home," or "You're too young to ask about that."*

Children between the ages of two and six sometimes handle their sex parts. It is normal and natural. If they do it very often, it may mean they are tense and worried, and you can then seek help in finding and removing the cause. Usually it is because the activity fills an idle moment, it feels good, or the little boy just wants to make certain his penis is still there. Or, they may do so merely because they have to go to the bathroom. Toys, games, play, and conversation are healthy substitutes. But it's wrong to tell him he'll hurt himself, he's bad, or you won't love him anymore, or to slap or tie his hands. The only real harm in the practice is making the young child feel guilty, ashamed, or frightened when he is doing what comes naturally to him.

RULE #4: *If your youngster masturbates occasionally, but has many interests and seems happy, try to involve the child in something else, but don't make a big deal over it.*

Getting a child off to a healthy attitude toward sex may be difficult for parents who themselves think there is something shameful about it; who don't know or are afraid to use the correct words to describe bodily parts or functions; or who see sex as something completely separate from love and a warm family feeling. The young child is usually satisfied with a few facts—told in simple words and without embarrassment by parents who love the youngster.

Keep Prejudice out of Your Family

- Under a South Seas moon the young Marine officer sang softly, thinking of his dark-skinned, beautiful island-sweetheart: "You've got to be taught to hate and fear…It's got to be drummed in your dear little ear…Before you are six or seven or eight, to hate all the people your relatives hate."
- A little white girl saw a black person for the first time, and she wondered if her teacher's face was "dirty."
- Television has become wide open to the hostility some of us feel and show toward others, playing with the subject for laughs.

As parents we have a chance to make our children "special" in a way never tried before on a large scale. The target is "prejudice," and evidence shows we can reduce it. Despite the music of "Carefully Taught" in *South Pacific*, a child-teacher relationship, and shows like *All in the Family*, we often bring our families very little related to this area so important to our children and their future. One authority in the field saw it this way:

Clearly this is one of our most, if not the most, serious of social problems… To continue to ignore this problem (as, relatively speaking, we have been doing) or to minimize it, is to invite disaster.

Let's look for a moment at the "clean slate" theory of infancy. Although babies are born with certain traits or tendencies, none of them aims toward dislike of other people. As in "Carefully Taught" it's through the almost constant drumming in the ears and minds of children growing up that we plant the seeds of dislike, distrust, and even hatred.

One scary study in a nice, clean-cut small midwestern community quoted children saying, "Kill them all" and "The only good one is a dead one" — and they were talking about minority groups not even living in their town! Their families, schools, churches, and community apparently didn't help battle such prejudices.

Rejection of playmates on the basis of race or religion is rare among preschool children, but something then happens to many of them. The "something" appears to be some of us, the adults who fill them with thoughts about people that are not true. One story on this subject made the rounds a few years ago.

It started with a mother hearing from another woman at a bridge party that the first one's young son had a new friend. He happened to be black, and it occurred to the mother that maybe she ought to check into it.

"Johnny, tell me about Bill, that new friend of yours," she said when she greeted him after school.

"Oh, he's great!" was the reply. "Runs faster than anybody. Catches a ball real good. And smart in school, too."

"But is there anything different about him?" the mother pressed. The little boy was puzzled and didn't answer.

"Well, is his skin a different color? Is he black?"

The boy paused, and then thoughtfully replied, "I don't know. I'll have to look tomorrow."

Perhaps the most vital part of this subject is the parents' point of view. Is it important enough to do something about it? If you feel that it is—that racial conflict and religious prejudice are worth fighting—you can act to keep it out of your family.

It's a tough task even for alert parents. Many of us are products of our own prejudice-building childhood. Our negative attitudes toward others may come out in subtle ways — "That's the way 'they' are" or "What can you expect?" or a knowing glance, a raised eyebrow, or a descriptive word that brings the deep feeling open.

Your self-control is needed so that such attitudes don't rub off. That's more useful than an occasional visit to the inner city or to "where the Mexicans, Blacks, and Native Americans live" and lectures and films about prejudice. Such hit-or-miss efforts aren't getting the job done.

A parent's opinion based on "I've-made-up-my-mind. Don't-bother-me-about-facts" can lead only to more of the most distasteful feelings among people. It's how *we* act and talk that helps develop sound attitudes in our children. Our preschoolers deserve a better world. After all, they haven't been dirtied by prejudice—yet.

Is it True What "They Say" About Young Children?

Parents read and hear many things about young children from research and "experts." The statements may sound so true and reasonable that parents sometimes begin to adopt them as their own. Here are some that need correction. They can even be bad for a small child if they are used carelessly.

- *"He's so wild…must be hyperactive!"* Is the child two…three…four…or five? If he can't be and act "immature" when he is so young, when can he? An educational film some years ago talked about the "terrible twos" and the "frustrating fours." Those words describe some children who act out, demand our time and patience, and wear us down. However, that does not mean we should use the label "hyperactive." It has become too easy in recent years to think of normal, active early childhood in such terms—and it is dangerous to do so. Such thoughts sometimes even lead to unnecessary sedatives.

  Just because the little child runs into the street, pulls up flowers, refuses to eat or sleep, or cuts a few curls from her hair does not mean she is "hyperactive." Although such children may not be easy to live with, this labeling might create far more problems than it solves. Yes, there *are* "hyperactive" and potentially "learning disabled" young children, many of them, but not the large numbers that has become almost fashionable to identify (falsely) and program (poorly) in some communities.

- *"They just play here. I want my child to learn something."* Play is the work and language of children. Through it they learn skills, build vocabularies, and solve problems. It all starts when a child is very young, in infancy, seeing the differences in sounds, colors, smells, tastes, and textures, and goes on through childhood games and sports. An activity need not be drudgery and drill for a child to learn. "The days that make us happy make us wise." Just because something is fun certainly doesn't mean we cannot learn from it. What a child gets through pleasure may be remembered much longer than what is learned through pain.

- *"Her speech is so hard to understand. I'm going to get help for her...therapy."* A young child may have hesitant speech, but that is probably not "stuttering." The child may not pronounce "l's" or r's" (saying "yady" for "lady" and "wabbit" for "rabbit"), but a child learns to say sounds accurately when ready and not before. They certainly do not all come out correctly at the same time. A parent who speaks clearly and uses the right words to describe what the child saw, did, wants, or likes can become a good model for a child. One who mumbles words or thinks it is cute to use "baby talk" shouldn't be surprised if a preschooler does the same.

- *"Nonprofit, public preschools are good for children. Others are in it just for the money."* If you visit many preschools you will see how wrong that statement can be. So-called "nonprofit" ones run the full range from excellent to disastrous—and so do the ones that are proprietary (for profit). Fine people and programs are seen in some of both, and so are unqualified teachers and unhappy, dirty settings. Besides, preschools in both groups make money or lose it. The key question is not whether it is for profit or nonprofit. Far more important are these: What do you do with and for my child? How well qualified are the teachers—in preparation, personality, and attitudes? What programs, equipment, and meals does the school have? Is it safe and healthy? May I visit? What does it cost?

Some things about young children *are* true, however. They are all different from each other, constantly surprise us with how much they know, say, and ask about (if we'll only take the time to listen), and can teach us so much about joy, happiness, and laughter—three needs that most of us sometimes have in such short supply!

Your Child is Special

The Young Gifted Child

Many parents are sure that their young children are bright—but it is so easy to be wrong. Because they say clever things, put words together in unusual ways, and ask questions that may be hard for you to answer, you might think they are gifted. After all, if a child asks, "What makes the sky blue?" or "What makes thunder?" doesn't that mean he's very smart?

The problem parents face is that they often don't see their youngster in comparison with others. The child may seem so quick—but others might be faster. So here's a checklist which can help you tell whether your preschool child is gifted. It is not necessary to score high on all 20 points, but if your youngster is strong on at least half of them, you can be quite sure she is bright.

Is Your Child Gifted?
- Started to walk and talk before most other children you know about
- Is at least a little taller, heavier, and stronger than others his or her age
- Shows an interest in time—clocks, calendars, yesterday and tomorrow, and days of the week
- Learned to read even though not yet five years old, likes to read
- Arranges toys and other possessions, putting the same kinds of things together
- Knows which numbers are larger than others
- Can count, and point to each item while correctly saying the number
- Creates make-believe playmates while "playing house" or different games
- Is interested in what is on television and in newspapers, in addition to cartoons and comics
- Learns easily, so that you have to tell him or her something only once
- Shows impatience with jobs around the house that seem to have no

meaning—like putting toys away when he is just going to have to take them out again

- Asks, "Why?" often, and really wants to know the answer; is curious about a lot of things, from a tiny insect and how it's "made" to a car and how it works
- Doesn't like to wait for other children to catch up
- Sticks with a task longer than others do; won't give up easily
- Does things differently and in ways that make good sense, whether it's piling up blocks, setting the table, or drying dishes
- Likes to be with older children, and can keep up with them
- Collects things, likes to organize them, and doesn't want anyone to mess them up—but doesn't always collect neatly
- Can carry on a conversation, and enjoys it. Wants your ideas and likes you to listen to his or hers; uses big words and knows what they mean
- Shows an interest in drawing and music, knows colors, and has rhythm
- Makes up jokes; has a good sense of humor

What should you do about it? How does your preschool youngster come out on that list? Strong enough so that you feel the child is gifted? All right—then are you ready for the next step? Before going on, try to make up your own list of what to do. Write in this book or on another sheet of paper. Cover up the rest of this page until you do.

Did your list include these: Talk about what she does, likes, and thinks; listen to her; read to her; take her places; enroll her in the best preschool, nursery school, or day care center you can find and afford. And when she goes to school, try to find the most creative, brightest teachers for her. Your list, and mine, may make you think about something interesting—These are, of course, the same things that parents should do for all their young children.

The Young Hyperactive Child

Some parents think their young child is hyperactive when he is merely doing what comes naturally. Two-, three-, and four-year-olds are often hard to live with. It is "normal" once in a while for them to have tantrums, move quickly from one toy or game to another, or wake up in the middle of the night. We should not call children "hyperactive" unless they *really* are, not just showing behavior that is usual for their age and development.

Characteristics. Are they *more* restless, difficult to get along with, and disruptive than other children of the same age? Do they cry, squirm, or fight more than others? Do they act in strange ways that they can't explain and you don't understand? Do they show little control over themselves and never seem to listen—but between times may be so sweet and lovable?

Other children are sometimes excitable and seem uncontrollable—but not most of the time. Others are sometimes sleepless, nervous, disorganized, or moody—but not almost all day or every night.

Hyperactive children often look like others. Their physical examinations seldom show any major differences. They are not mentally retarded although due to their unusual behavior, they may do less well than others in playing games, completing little household chores, or listening to a story. They are not "bad" because they want to be, but they often act in ways that most adults don't like or can't accept.

Causes. Experts don't always give the same reason for why a certain youngster is hyperactive. However, they usually agree that more boys than girls are. A child "acts out" because he has a neurological disease or disorder...or had a childhood sickness or accident...or lives with or apart from arguing, separated, unloving, or uncaring parents...or never receives praise...or is hurt or rejected physically or emotionally. Add to that list difficulties of mother or child before birth or injuries at birth and you have most of the reasons why a child may be hyperactive.

What to do about it. Hyperactivity is a symptom and not a cause. To eliminate or reduce it, the cause should be identified (if possible) and minimized. You may not be able to do it alone; you may need assistance from a physician and a skilled nursery or day care teacher.

If your child is mildly hyperactive, preschool encouragement and supervised play may be helpful. If your child is severely hyperactive, you shouldn't expect teachers to provide one-to-one help. You'll need the necessary combination of medical, psychological, and psychiatric support. Your own doctor may be the place to start. However, the first approach to the problem should begin even earlier, at home. Among the specific things you can provide are these:

- A structured routine of dressing, meals, and cleanliness
- Keeping the bedroom in order, with your help
- Tasks at which the child can succeed, and rewards for success
- Consistent discipline that makes sense to the child
- Time you schedule alone with the child
- A substitute for mother or father if either one is missing
- A record of your child's behavior: when, where, and under what circumstances the hyperactivity occurs

Drugs or other medication may be necessary, but only if other means don't work and a physician recommends them. Some possible side effects to drugs may develop, including being depressed or withdrawn. That's one of the reasons for research on other kinds of controls, like removing artificial food coloring and flavoring and giving the child coffee. Such research is still in process. Most children outgrow hyperactivity to at least some extent by adolescence. However, it is sometimes easier on the family if drugs (under supervision) are used in the pre-adolescent years.

Whether a child is called "hyperactive," "hyperkinetic," or "minimal brain damaged," the child needs your help, and the earlier the better. Otherwise, school failure or emotional disturbances may come. Some of these later difficulties might be avoided if you recognize the problems while your child is young, provide the environment that includes both structure and love, and seek professional assistance when necessary.

The Young Shy Child

Timid…withdrawn…quiet…easily frightened…do words like those describe the young child in your family? If they do, join the crowd, for they describe preschool children in many families. A more important question is this one: *How often* and *in what situations* is your youngster shy? If your answer is "Always," "Frequently," or "In most situations," your first step may be to talk to the child's preschool teacher or pediatrician for advice or referral to a family counselor or other expert.

Chances are that the shyness or timidity that worries you happens only once in a while—and both the cause and solutions are easy to identify. When does your child show such tendencies? Afraid to climb or jump…wants to play alone…avoids loud noises and loud children…hides behind you when strangers come up…fearful of big animals or dark places? You can probably add other situations to that list.

First, let's recognize that it is normal to avoid situations that are not pleasant. We do it as adults, don't we? Grown-ups may also not like high places, crowds, noise, meeting new people, darkness, and threatening animals. We sometimes push our young children before they are ready. A child may prefer the bottom of the slide for a while or the chance to watch rather than join the group. Maybe we ought to hold ourselves back, wait for the "teachable moment," say "I'll catch you if you want to jump." Calm, relaxed encouragement rather than pressing too hard too soon is much more pleasing for both youngster and parent.

We might cause the so-called shyness in other ways, too. Constant warnings ("Be careful!" "Watch out!" "Don't fall!" "Hold on tightly!") often create timidity. Trial-and-error (and even an occasional bruise) is better, although you certainly want to prevent unnecessary accidents and danger. That's what fences and locks on windows are for. We also can create timidity by being too strict, not letting a child run, climb, and jump when the desire is there. The child may not try again if you show you don't like the idea; because your approval is important, a little child may think, "Why buck the boss?"

A frightening experience (whether it is from a barking dog, a loud stranger, or a near auto accident) is usually remembered only a short time, and the timidity that results may pass quickly—if your reaction is calm, relaxed, and sympathetic. That's asking a lot of a parent who might be excitable and easily worried. Little children are overwhelmed by adults who hug too soon or sympathize too often and long.

We may bring on shyness when we push a child toward being the center of attention, showing "good manners" in meeting people, or becoming part of a group. Our pressure may force the youngster to withdraw. Gentle waiting might take longer, but it's easier on the child in the long run.

Children are different (even within the same family), and so are their tendencies toward shyness or timidity. Families differ, too—loud or quiet, outgoing or withdrawn—and children reflect those differences. If we look ahead for a moment, we'll recognize that the adult jobs our young children will later occupy require varied personality characteristics. The ability to work alone in a laboratory is as "normal" as the desire to be "on-stage" in front of a classroom or audience. So a respected future job may be waiting for your quiet, reserved, non-aggressive child. Forcing youngsters to "group it up" may not fit in with their needs and personalities. However, alert parents will provide both the opportunity and subtle encouragement so their children will be at ease with others and in most non-threatening situations. To comfortably face (rather than hide from) people and pressures is one of the important goals most of us have for our children.

"Fragile" or "Strong"—
Which Describes Your Child?

An expert on children once described them by telling a story about three dolls. One was made of glass, the second of plastic, and the third of steel. Each was hit by a hammer. The first one broke, the second was bent, and the third gave off a beautiful, metallic sound. Perhaps all of our children fit into that story, reacting in different ways to the same event or pressure.

Some parents yell, and their children begin to learn the difference between right and wrong. When other parents scream, their children may stop listening, get turned off, and learn something, but not what their parents might expect; they learn to escape the screaming, hide from it, ignore it.

Most of us try to give our children the best possible start in life. Our precious money, valuable time, and whatever patience we can spare go into their early years because we realize how important they are. Still, a disturbing thought may have occurred to you. Perhaps you know some people who have done "everything" for their children, and they get little in return—their youngsters may choose the wrong friends, do poorly in school, have no goals for today, tomorrow, or their future, and show no love or respect.

Others couldn't care less about their children, permit them to roam without permission, seem to devote no thought to what they wear or eat, and neither speak nor listen to them. You'd think the result would be complete failure, a child without hope or affection. But it doesn't always turn out like that.

As important as the early years are, as much as we try to do for and with our youngsters, and as concerned as we are about what kind of people they will grow up to be, once in a while we should remember this vital fact: *As parents we have little control over some of the strengths and weaknesses with which our children are born and some of the influences on their lives outside of your family and home environments. We cannot take credit for all they do which makes us feel proud any more than we can or should always take the blame when things go wrong.*

Have you ever read or heard about the early childhoods of Eleanor Roosevelt, Thomas Edison, and Albert Einstein? They were far from ideal. If you tried to guess how they would turn out as adults on the basis of their young years, you might assume they would be failures. Yet they were exactly the opposite in the contributions they made.

You may know some children—one of them might even be your own—who live under almost constant pressure and stress, deprived of a good diet, a comfortable home, and the warmth of a family where love is part of every day. Yet they thrive and grow up strong even when deprived of what seem like the most basic needs. They are very different from the fragile child who fails even though his or her parents do, buy, read, take, and encourage, all without success. Some children born into extreme poverty (of ideas and love as well as money) "make it"; others with all the support that money can buy might fail. The reasons for both may be outside the hands and controls of parents.

So what does all that add up to? Does it mean that children will profit from abuse? Of course not, but it does indicate that *some* children can survive even the most negative parts of their environment and perhaps will be like the steel doll, neither broken nor scarred by the blows it receives.

There is no special joy in suffering. Young children seldom gain from it, and as adults we know that. Just because some of them have the fantastic strength to survive disaster certainly doesn't mean we should deliberately seek it out for them The road to success is filled with mud puddles, a wise educator once said. Some children jump over and others fall in. As parents we can help them do either one.

Help Your Children Talk Better

No one is able to talk at birth. What young children say and how they say it is learned during their first few years. And they learn mainly by imitation and because they need and want things. They hear you, their brothers and sisters, and playmates. They find out that they can get a toy or a piece of candy by asking for it. If parents want to help their children talk better they should speak and listen to them, beginning in infancy and through the preschool years.

For most children speech is acquired in this order: Infancy—sounds and babbling; by age one—the first words; by age two—words combined into simple sentences; by age three—sentences with three to five words; by age four—more complete sentences and questions. But some children reach these stages at different times, and they may be just as "normal." Nothing is necessarily wrong because they are a little slower than others are. Nor do they all learn to speak clearly in these early years. Far from it! Among the sounds that come first and are usually easiest for them are p, b, m, and n. Later come t, g, d, and k. And still later (sometimes not until youngsters are five or six) they may begin to correctly use l, f, s, and r and combinations like sh, st, th, tr, and bl. To check out your own young children, listen how they pronounce words like "stop," "rabbit," "thumb," "black," "train," and "lady."

Most children do not master all the sounds until they are at least seven- or eight-years-old. Young children often hesitate, repeat, and stumble over their words, but they are probably not "stuttering." Haven't you ever found it difficult to talk smoothly about an important topic to someone who's not interested? Youngsters frequently face the blank wall of parental disinterest. It doesn't help to tell them, "You can say it better…Try again…Talk slowly…Say it already." It may help a great deal more to talk clearly and calmly yourself and to avoid as many tense, frustrating situations for them as you can. To label the normal speech of three- and four-year-olds as "stuttering" could lead to actual stuttering. A child may then need special help for many years to overcome it.

There are several reasons why preschool children do not speak clearly. The main one is that they haven't developed the necessary skills. Others are talking "baby talk" to the child and not conversing enough with your youngsters. Less frequent causes of early hard-to-understand speech patterns are hearing problems and poor development of the complicated speech mechanism.

What parents can do about the speech and vocabulary of their preschool youngsters falls into two parts: You can help prevent difficulties; and you can help correct minor ones.

- *Prevention.* Do you let the child finish what she wants to say? Do you answer her questions (within reason!)? Do you sometimes try to echo back what she says but in expanded form? (If she says "shoe" or "more," you might respond, "Yes, your shoe is right here" or "Of course, you can have some more Jell-O.") Do you talk to her in full, short sentences, or just in sharp commands like "Wash your hands," "Eat," "Go to bed," and "Stop that right now!"? Do you really listen to what she is saying or just to how she says it?
- *Correction of minor difficulties.* Listen for indistinct sounds like "thoap" for "soap" and "fum" for "thumb." You and your youngster can then collect pictures of things that begin with those correct sounds. Say the words accurately and encourage him to do so. Praise him when he does. But try this activity only if you have the patience, and limit yourself to a few minutes a day.

Games based on rhyming words, "What's another way to say_____," and "How do you think the story ends?" (when reading) are other approaches you can use. You can help develop correct speech and build vocabulary in these important early years. In addition, a good preschool or nursery school has teachers who can help you expand on the suggestions offered here.

Learning Disabilities
(Some young children have them)

"Learning disabilities" has become a common label for many school-age children. It refers to learning habits that are delayed or seem mixed up or confused. Such problems are often ignored by parents and teachers for too long. The time for you to notice and start doing something about them (if they really exist) is during the preschool years. But first, you may need a little information:

- Behavior of some two-, three-, and four-year-olds that is hard to live with does not necessarily mean that they will have learning problems later on. Immature ways are normal for young children.
- Just because a youngster takes a little longer than others to learn some things—for example, riding a bike, putting together a puzzle, or learning the rules of a new game—doesn't mean the child is "learning disabled." We all learn at different rates.
- Children who have learning disabilities are usually of average or above-average intelligence. They are definitely not mentally challenged.

What seems strange or different to you might not to others who are more objective. Experienced day care and preschool teachers may be your best source for advice. Here are some characteristics that can help you tell whether a young child will have learning problems. If the child has one or two of them, it may not be important, but a combination of several could be.

- Is the child's behavior especially uncontrollable?
- Did the child start to walk late? How is coordination now (like catching a ball or copying or tracing simple designs)? Does the child often fall when running?

- Do people outside the family have difficulty understanding the child?
- Does she have a problem finding her toys and clothes even after you tell her many times?
- Does the child run off after a few seconds, rather than sticking with a task or game?
- Does the child frequently act tired or not interested, or seem to be afraid or worried, in connection with activities that other children enjoy?
- Is it difficult for the child to tell sounds apart—a bell from a buzzer, a tap from a clap, or words that rhyme?
- Do a square, a triangle, and a rectangle look the same to him? Can he tell them apart?
- Does he quickly forget what you've shown or told him?
- Is it difficult for her to tell that things feel differently, like various cloths, sandpaper and wood, or salt, coffee, and sugar? Can she tell one taste or smell from another?
- Is the child confused about the difference between up and down, over and under, and outside and inside?
- Does the child give the same answer, again and again, to different questions?

What should you do?
- Reduce distractions. Cut down the clutter and confusion around the child. For example, read stories away from the telephone and other conversations.
- Help give structure to his young life. Set limits that are reasonable. Be sure he understands them.
- Help her plan ahead. Keep plans simple. Concentrate on today, not next week. Well-organized time, space, and activities can reduce her confusion.
- Try not to put the child "in the middle" between parents or other adults. Agree in advance about what the child will do and when.
- Praise your child freely, but don't use fake compliments.
- Encourage her to do things at which she can succeed.
- Involve the child in activities that can help him become orderly, like setting the table, putting groceries away, and sorting laundry.
- Have fun with differences and similarities: sweet and sour tastes; various smells; textures that feel different; colors, sizes, and shapes that look different; loudness and other variations in sound.
- Give one direction at a time. Use short sentences and simple words.

If your child actually has learning disablity, the earlier you discover and help correct the problem the better. School people probably will later on anyway, but why lose valuable time?

Preparing Your Child for School

Every Child is Creative

Children lose part of their creativity by the time they are five. That's what some research says. But do they really have to? Can you do something to help your youngsters retain the curiosity, eagerness to explore and learn, and imagination of the first few years? Yes, you certainly can. And it costs very little in time and money.

Because a child's areas of enjoyment are so numerous, many parents get scared off. "What do I know about animals, gardening, and magnets?...I'm a dud at music, dancing, and art...Let the schools do it." What parents can do to encourage creativity isn't really difficult. Here are a few examples:

- Young children like to use their bodies—jump, rock, dance, sway, creep, skip, and walk in funny ways, using their heads, hands, arms, and legs. So let music come into your house through records, radio, television, or instruments.

- Young children like to make things, sometimes using tools and brushes. They like to feel different materials and squeeze them through their fingers. So once in a while provide clay, scraps of soft wood, colored paper, and even paint, sand, and mud. It'll all wash off! Some items aren't safe and some stain, so that's where your adult judgment has to come in.

- Young children like to make believe. So give them puppets, grown-up clothes, and other props from which they'll create a whole new world of magic and fantasy. You might be an audience for them occasionally—you might even enjoy the show.

- Young children like to rhyme sounds and words, tell stories, and compose songs and poems. So encourage them—and once in a while leave the TV or newspaper and listen to them. Use waiting moments in grocery stores, doctors' offices, and traffic delays, and don't be too upset with what may seem like silly behavior. If they can't "let themselves go" when they're two, three, or four, when can they?

A walk in the rain, a seed planted in a window box, a magnifying glass, a thank-you letter to grandma, a castle made with blocks—the ideas for creative growth are all around us. They extend to your own interest areas, too. Young children like nothing better than to be included in your activities and hobbies, even if it's cooking, auto repair, or carpentry.

Three cautions are important: don't be "sexist" (girls can use a hammer, boys may like to play house, and both activities are good starts toward meeting later needs); don't expect too much (preschoolers' sewing may need adult assistance, for example); don't set firm patterns or models for them to follow (it isn't necessary that they paint within strict lines).

To help children keep and expand the creativity of their early years requires parent understandings like these:

- Recognize that everything is new for them. "Everything" includes the sky, clouds, rain, stars, and wind, and extends to tiny insects, pebbles, snowflakes, and leaves that most adults seldom notice. After all, small children are often a couple of feet closer to them than we are!
- Accept the idea that the exciting world comes to them through their eyes, but also through sounds, tastes and smells, and by way of their finger tips, too.
- Realize that we must show interest to help them retain theirs, but it's foolish to fake it. Most children, even young ones, are alert to parents' acting as though they enjoy childhood games when they're really a bore to them.
- Emphasize that the pictures they draw, the sounds and words they create, and the body movements they make are their very own. They are as much theirs, and theirs alone, as their fingerprints are.

Preschool teachers can provide many additional ideas. If you want to treat yourself to an exciting view of a young child's world and how you can help him retain that view as he grows older, locate a copy of Rachel Carson's *The Sense of Wonder* (Harper and Row). All parents of preschool children could benefit from her point of view based on happiness through discovery. Because some school restrictions may soon close in on your youngster, it's especially important to use these early years, which pass so quickly, to help establish the habit of creativity.

Off to a Good Start in Arithmetic

Will your preschool youngster be good at arithmetic when he gets to school? Will he like it? How he feels about it may depend on how you do. If it's hard or dull for you, it may be for him, too. But it doesn't have to be. Some children get off to an unhappy start in arithmetic because they are forced to count and read or write numbers before counting and numbers really mean anything to them.

Try this: Place ten coins in front of your three- or four-year-old child, and ask her to count them. Maybe she will point to the first one or two, and say the right numbers, but from then on she may be all wrong. That's normal. She might be ready to begin learning about numbers even though she can't always use them correctly.

You can help prepare your child to use numbers later on by making size, shape, direction, and likenesses and differences a part of your everyday conversations and not a special thing. When you are with your young child as he is getting dressed, taking a bath, walking to nursery school, riding in a car, or going grocery shopping, you can build toward numbers and counting. Both of you can enjoy it, too. Here are some easy beginnings:

Size. Using crayons, pencils, balls, silverware, dishes, and members of the family, talk and ask about which is largest, smallest, longest, or shortest. Make a game of looking for the biggest and littlest articles in his room, the backyard, or on the playground. Help him see that there is more milk in this glass than in that cup, and less ice cream in the bowl after he has eaten part of it.

Shape. She can play with squares, circles, triangles, and other designs that she sees in blocks or that you cut out of cardboard. You might get down on the floor and help fit them together. Shapes and designs are all around us—

balloons, billboards, road signs, everywhere. You can help your child see them, but she is able to discover a lot about them by herself, too.

Direction. Talk to him about pictures, leaves, flowers, birds, and toys that are above, below, inside, outside, or on something else. When you drive or turn to the right or left, you might sometimes tell him that you are.

Likenesses and differences. Help her put things together that belong together, like her socks, cans of food, buttons, and pictures of animals. She will begin to see that some are the same, and others are different. Point out other differences, too—for example, in the height of children, the speed of automobiles and ants, the weight of rocks, cotton, and sand, and the cost of candy and clothing.

Don't leave numbers out entirely, of course. Count with him when you clap hands, bounce a ball, and set the table. Count with him as he points to objects in a row or as he goes up or down steps. Usually you can't go beyond five or ten with your preschool child, although he might be bright and able to do so.

Talk about two hands, two feet, two shoes, and two eyes. The idea of "five fingers," and a "few children," "some candy," "many people," and "all the toys" will come easily just a little later.

Ideas related to size, shape, direction, and likenesses and differences should be kept simple. Although one well-known man said that any subject (including arithmetic) can be taught to anybody at any age, you and your youngster will enjoy it more if you take it easy, without pushing too hard. Try not to be too serious about all of this. Your preschool child will learn most about the early stages of arithmetic as she experiments with blocks and toys, alone and with her friends.

You can get other ideas about the beginnings of numbers, counting and arithmetic from: your youngster's preschool teacher; a good toy store with inexpensive toys based on sizes, shapes, and patterns; and the best children's television shows.

Science and the Young Child

An expert in how children learn once wrote that children can be taught any subject at any age. Although he no doubt should have made some exceptions (low-performing, mentally challenged children, for example), he is basically correct. Children can learn a lot more, and earlier, than we often expect. By using all of their senses, young ones constantly explore this new, wonderful world of theirs. What they see, hear, taste, smell, and touch may tell them more in their first five years than some of them learn later in school. When newspaper people write a news article they cover the five W's and an H—Who, What, Where, When, Why, and How. Your preschooler asks the same questions. If your patience can match that curiosity, a lot of learning will take place.

Sometimes children ask questions just to hear their own voice and that leads to another story. One father of a little boy did what so many of us do when the questions come: He hid behind the sports section of the evening paper. The child's questions were, "What makes the grass green?...Why is the sky blue?... Where is the sun at night?" The bored, muffled answer was always the same, "I don't know." After all the turndowns the youngster stormed out of the room, screaming, "I won't ask you anything...ever, ever again!"—finally grabbing the father's attention. Putting down the paper, he yelled back, "You have to ask questions! How are you going to learn things otherwise?"

So much of a young child's life has the same qualities—searching, wondering, investigating, examining—as the questions that the child asks. Young children are scientists, and we can help them get and continue the habit of exploring, seeking an answer to the question we often still ask as adults... "Why?" Science activities you can use with a preschool child cost little or nothing, but they may take a bit of time. Here are some examples. Your child's preschool teacher can probably suggest many others.

- Take a walk, look at trees, talk about them. Identify colors and compare leaves.
- Put a sweet potato in a glass of water; watch its vines and roots grow. Place carrot tops in two dishes of water; after they start growing, cover one completely with a jar. Is air important?
- Study shadows at different times of day. Get a prism and observe the colors. Use a magnet.
- Study the parts of an insect. Watch the fish in your aquarium. Why does your cat or dog act as it does?
- Ask "What if?" questions. What would happen if we could fly, had just one eye, everything were the same color, it never rained? You'll have a good time making up others.
- Ask questions yourself, like "Why is it hot (or cold) outside? Why does it get dark at night? Why do we get hungry (or sleepy, angry, or happy)?" In case you can't provide the answers in simple, understandable terms, it's a good idea to check them out first.
- Study together the inside of an old clock, discuss why a tall tower of blocks falls over, talk about why people lose their teeth or hair.
- Plant seeds...Fly a kite...Go to the zoo...Visit a farm, a factory, a bakery...Cook together.

In her fine book, *The Sense of Wonder*, Rachel Carson points out that parents don't need a lot of knowledge to steer a young child toward a science track. You don't have to be an expert.

Just one more thought...has it ever occurred to you why a young child is so interested in inspecting things closely (like a flower, a snowflake, or a blade of grass) and runs back and forth checking on them? One reason is that the child is closer to them than we are, a few feet closer. Another is that it's all so new. Wouldn't it be great if we could have kept some of that excitement in our own lives? Let's try to help our children keep at least part of it in theirs.

Too Young to Learn Thinking Skills? No!

Don't you wish that all the people with whom you live and work could think clearly...accurately...logically? Maybe *some* of them can! Do you know one of the main reasons why you perhaps run into so many fuzzy thinkers? It may be that they just didn't learn how to organize their ideas early enough.

Your preschool child is at the age when you should help in pulling ideas together in an orderly way, as well as guiding toward new ones. You may not make your youngster brighter, more intelligent, but the child may *seem* brighter because of an ability to put thoughts together in a sensible way. To increase your young child's thinking skills, the following suggestions may be helpful:

- Realize that the more experiences a child has the easier it becomes to think through problems...the more a child has to figure things out, the more he is able to solve problems of the same type.
- Bring up new ideas but not completely strange ones. They should be related in some way to what your child already knows and understands. Present play, toy, and home activities can be the starting point.
- Provide practice in looking for small details in pictures and stories, and talk about them together.
- Use small doses of new information. Young children can easily be overwhelmed by too much too fast. After all, there will be other times and other days.
- Involve your youngster through seeing, touching, hearing, smelling, and tasting. Talking "at" her isn't enough. A famous educator was on the right track when he stressed "learning by doing." It's better than just watching and listening.
- Use correct names for what your preschooler experiences, and encourage him to use them, too.

- Expect to repeat what you say. You didn't learn everything the first time either!
- Encourage conversation, but correcting grammar can get in the way. Although "her did it," "he holded them," and "nobody don't come" may bother you, it is the idea that you want even more than perfect grammar.
- Ask questions to extend a child's thoughts, but try not to fake them. It is best if you are honestly seeking information through questions like "What did you do then?" "What else does it look like?" "What color is it?" and "Which one is larger?"
- Remember it takes time to understand words and ideas like the following, but you can help provide the needed practice: more, less; below, above, under, on, inside, outside; before, after; big, bigger, biggest.
- Use different words and full sentences to help broaden vocabulary and conversation. Her "shoe," "see," or "give me" can expand to your "Yes, this shoe right here," "Let's look at your book together," or "What would you like me to give you?"
- Realize that no child is equally alert and attentive at all times. There is such a thing as "the teachable moment," and a sleepy, over-excited, or distressed youngster isn't ready for it even though *you* may be.

Experiences that can develop thinking skills include figuring out which things go together or are used together (like tools, eating utensils, flowers, odors, and animals) and finding what is similar or different (as among playing cards, buttons, nails, and boxes, sorting by size, color, or design). Take a few minutes to listen to children talk about what and why they are classifying, sorting, or whatever else excites or interests them.

Neither you nor even a fine preschool teacher can provide all the experiences young children need to sharpen their thinking skills. They seek them out on their own, on the playground, in the doll corner, in their own rooms. A youngster's thinking can mature without formal teaching, but you can help when you see that the child is ready for new words and ideas.

There are no magic ways to produce high intelligence. However, you can provide the environment at home and in a well-selected preschool to develop doing, asking, talking, and other skills that contribute to a child's maturity—and also to reasoning and problem-solving skills that we all need as adults.

Your Young Child's Language

A recognized expert on intelligence testing (Dr. L. M. Terman) once said that vocabulary is the best single indication of how bright a child is. However, that bit of information doesn't usually help parents much. We are not often objective about our own children. To us what they say is so clever, bright, and creative. A good preschool teacher sees our small child with others and therefore can be more accurate in judging how well our youngster's language is developing.

Learning to speak and understand what others say begins at birth. A baby's babbling and cooing is a first effort toward communicating. What you say and your tone of voice will be imitated. Infants—as well as older children—also tell us a great deal through "body language." Their hands, facial expressions, even their toes tell us what they want and how they feel. So do their tears, clinging hugs, and sleeplessness.

As your child's first and most important teacher, you can help develop communication skills that in adulthood often separate those who succeed from those who don't "make it." Here's a checklist of ideas for you to consider.

- Did you *talk* to your youngster even before the child could reply with words? Do you now?
- Do you *listen*, really listen, concentrate on *what* is said and *how* it is said? Can you keep from interrupting?
- Does your *conversation* evolve out of something that you or your youngster is doing (rather than through setting up a special time to converse)—while doing everyday things like sorting laundry, washing dishes, shopping, setting the table, or what and whom you see on the way to the preschool?
- Do you welcome *questions* (up to a point!), answer them, ask some back, but not just the "yes" and "no" type? Do you aim for longer answers with

questions like "What did you eat...what toys did you play with...what did you do with them?" (Caution: Restrain yourself. No one likes to be attacked by a steady flow of questions.)

- Do you *read* and *watch television* with your young child—and then talk about what you read or saw?
- Do you *compliment, encourage, reward, show pleasure and excitement— honestly?* "That's a good idea!"..."Great!"...and "You did such a good job" make sense only if you're telling the truth.
- How about discussing *colors*, using words that *rhyme*, talking about *what will or may happen next in a story, describing pictures*, and using *directional words* (like under, over, in, out, above, below, around)?
- Are you able to correct language without seeming to—as when a child says, "I never had a *funner* time" your reply could be, "I'm so glad you enjoyed yourself." If their language or ideas seem immature to you, it may be worth asking yourself: When can they be healthfully immature if not when they're two, three, four, or five?
- Do you fully understand that words mean different things to each of us, especially with young children—obvious ones like "money" and "death," and less apparent ones like "clean," "pretty," and "yes/no."
- How often do you schedule time with *one child alone?*

We sometimes forget that there is more than one vocabulary—the one consisting of words they *understand*, another used when they *speak*, and two others developed later when they *read* and *write*. Our objective should be to expand all of them through all of the senses—*sight, hearing, touch, taste*, and *smell*. The more experiences they have with you away from and at home and at their preschool, the broader their vocabulary will become.

Let's be specific: What did you do with your young child during *the most important five minutes of the day* yesterday—right after you came home from work? What will you do with him or her tonight? What you do for yourself to relax from the tensions of the day is crucial for you, of course. But it is for a little child, too.

Helping Your Child get Ready to Read

Can you help your preschool child get ready to read? Is it worthwhile? Can it contribute to, rather than interfere with, the actual teaching of reading later on in school? The answer is "Yes" to all three questions.

This enjoyable experience for you and your youngster requires no special preparation and very little time. What you can do is based on three items, and your child already has a strong start in all of them: *listening, seeing,* and *words.* Some fancy educational labels say almost the same thing: auditory discrimination and memory; visual discrimination and memory; and vocabulary or language development. Stated more simply, they add up to giving the child greater experiences with the sounds, sights, and words that are around every day. Here are just a few examples of the many activities through which you can help him get ready to read. If you ask your youngster's preschool teacher, you will no doubt get many additional suggestions.

Listening
- *Following instructions.* Start with one, and gradually add others. Does the child pay attention while you're talking? Stick with a job until it's finished? Do you tell the child how well she did it?
- *Sounds.* Ask the child, "What sound does a snake (or train, plane, or sheep) make?" "Close your eyes, and make the same sound I make (p...b...m...s...t...d)." "Do these words sound the same?...or how are they different?" (Examples are "boy...toy," "rug...hug," "see...me.")
- *Hearing games.* Remind the child that it may seem perfectly quiet, but there are sounds around us. "What do you hear?" Or ask him, with his eyes closed, "Tell me what you hear." (Drop the keys, slam a door, run water, type, use the vacuum cleaner.) "What word rhymes with...?" (Use common ones like "rose," "cat," "tree," and "cow.")

Seeing

- *Eye test*. Have your child's eyes examined by a competent person. This is a basic step in getting the child ready to read.
- *Missing items*. Put out three or four objects (pencils, buttons, erasers, spoons, etc.) and ask the child to close his eyes. Remove one—"Which one is missing?" Have him shut his eyes while you rearrange them— "Put them back as they were before."
- *Comparisons*. Use blocks, beads, pictures, or magnetized letters on your refrigerator. "How are they the same (different)?" "Which is bigger (or smaller, most, least, above, below, on, under, next to, inside, outside, behind)?" Use buttons, nails, and pieces of cloth to compare shapes, sizes, colors, and textures.
- *Drawing, puzzles, directions, copying*. Say, "That's a pretty tree (or truck). Can you draw it?" Encourage her to color within boundaries and to draw a line between other lines (straight, curved, angled) without touching them. Use cut-up pictures of faces, animals, or cars; puzzles are fun to put together. "Show me which way the car is going (or the lady is facing)." "Can you put these beads on a string as I do? Let's try."

Words

- *Games*. Ask the child, "What will happen if…" it rains today, Andy or Amy comes over to play, we stick a pin in a balloon, or plant these seeds?
- *Books*. Read to your child, even if it's for only a few minutes a day. Use the local library. Buy some books with lots of pictures and a few words. Help the child notice that pages go from front to back, top to bottom, and left to right. Ask, "How do you think this story ends?"—and as you go along, ask specific questions like, "What did the boy want?" and "What was the girl wearing?" Have him mention objects or events in illustrations that are also in the book.
- *Pictures*. Use them from television commercials, billboards, and grocery cans, asking, "What is it called?" "How do you think this happened?" (a wrecked car in a newspaper picture), "What is this? What caused it?" (a flood), "What do we have to do to get some?" (beautiful flowers)—such questions can help increase young vocabularies.

Don't feel you have to use all of these ideas—or that these are the only ones to use. A few may go a long way for you and your youngster. Too many questions and boredom are signs that you might be trying too hard. It's important to keep your eye on the right target—to increase your preschool child's listening, seeing, and word experiences. That goal can become a sound basis for competent and enjoyable reading in all the school years that lie ahead.

Reading with Your Young Child

Do you read to your young child? Some parents start when a child is two. Some begin even earlier. Others never do it because they feel they don't have time or it isn't important.

If you want your youngster to become a reader, to enjoy books, and to learn from them, you should be reading to him or her early. It will take only a few minutes each day, and it can help lead to a love for reading and toward a nice feeling for school and learning later on. Reading with a young child can be enjoyable for you, too. If you choose a story that is fun and a book with bright pictures, both of you can have a good time.

The list of books which youngsters like gets longer every year. You may be surprised at the many topics they cover and their colorful drawings and photographs. Almost any young child can become excited by fairy tales and stories about animals, other children, airplanes, and trains. These stories can help open up a big, new world. Here is a simple checklist you can use to help start this enjoyable activity.

- Select books your child will like. Get suggestions from a preschool teacher, children's librarian, or bookstore. These books don't have to cost much money—and those that come from the library with the child's own library card will probably cost nothing.
- Set up a daily schedule—like before bedtime or nap time, or after dinner. Be ready to change it sometimes, for important things such as being with a friend or having a snack.
- Notice if the child gets bored, tired, or cranky. Next time try to stop before that happens. Reading to children should always be a happy experience for both parent and child.

- Laugh together, wonder what will happen next, feel sorry if the child or animal in the story has a problem, and share a joyful ending when everything turns out all right.
- Read only part of a story once in a while and let your youngster finish telling it. Ask, "What do you think happened next?" or "What should the boy (or girl) do now?" Then finish reading it so the endings can be compared.
- Read clearly and slowly. Show you enjoy the story.
- Let older brothers and sisters help out. They may like to share your reading to a younger child.
- Use the pictures. Ask, "What is happening here?"
- Let your youngster ask questions. Try to answer them. Talk about the story after you are finished.
- Tell old familiar stories about the three bears, Little Red Riding Hood, and others, and then read them. The best ones are worth retelling and re-reading many times.
- Help your child begin a personal library. Let the child put his name in his books (with your assistance if necessary).
- Subscribe to one or more children's magazines, ordering them in her name.
- Let your child have quiet, free time to look at books alone.
- Use books to find out things. This starts the habit of looking up information.
- Buy books as presents sometimes, for your child and for others. Let the child choose them, unless they are to be a surprise.

Reading with young children isn't limited to books. There are traffic signs like Walk, School Zone, and Keep Right, labels on food, signs in stores, and television commercials. Don't make a big deal out of reading all these with children. A little bit can go a long way. Reading games can be fun, too. Being the first to see a motel sign or a favorite hamburger billboard can be part of the reading process.

Just as important as the reading you do with a young child is the example you set. Your reading and how much you enjoy it can help set the stage for the child's reading. Children learn by seeing you read from left to right, top to bottom, and front to back, and turn pages and use a proper light. But much more important is the fun of it now and the values toward which these few minutes a day can lead.

Dealing with
Life's Little Problems

Manners—Are They Important?

- "You're silly, Daddy!"
- Grandma brings a present, but there is no "Thank you."
- Spilled milk and sloppy eating
- Interruptions or a center-of-attention, "Look at me!" attitude

How do you handle situations like these with your young child? Do you ignore or punish…pass the buck to the other parent or to a preschool, or bear down hard to "be sure" it won't happen again? Perhaps you've made up your mind that manners are extremely important—or of no importance at all, but in either case read on for a few minutes. It's not quite that simple.

Times have changed, of course, and we've left far behind the formal teaching of manners based on "How d'you do?" and bowing slightly. Although as adults we are often more relaxed these days, some basic thoughts still apply to us—and to our young children:

- People resent those who are rude, inconsiderate, or unpleasant.
- We all want to be liked.
- We learn from the example of the company we keep. For young children that "company" is most frequently their own family.

Key words and attitudes within the family provide the pattern your youngster will follow. Speaking with a full mouth, constantly interrupting and without an "excuse me," and yelling or loud television when someone is trying to sleep are all easily copied by a young child—but so are the exact opposites. Good manners usually come almost naturally if a child sees or hears a respected adult practice them. Dad gives his seat on the bus to an older, handicapped, or ill person, or to one with heavy packages. An older brother or sister waits until everyone is served before eating. No one demands all the conversation time; there is sharing.

Although courtesy shown to others can be practiced at home, it's often so easy to be crude, even obnoxious, with those we know best! It may take a little effort for us to quiet down a bit, control the words we use, and practice the eating and other habits that we once learned but now sometimes forget. However, your young child is all eyes and ears—and you're the teacher! If you want to have a child who is easier to live with and accepted and liked by others, a few early childhood rules may be worth considering:

Table manners. To enjoy eating and feeding himself or herself (even if it's sometimes not so neat), talking and listening, and leaving the table when neither the food nor the conversation are of any further interest are more important than which fork to use. How to cut with a knife, handle a glass, and use a napkin will come with your example—and when you explain, quietly and perhaps several, maybe even many times.

Visitors in your home. We sometimes push a young child "on stage," to "do" or "say" something. A preschooler needs time to size up the stranger and will break in when ready, sometimes with a comment you don't expect, about the bathroom flood, the puppy's "accident," or what Daddy said about his boss. (However, comfortably sharing an experience is good manners, too.) Cookie passing, "show your new kitty," or a natural opening in the conversation may help involve your youngster. The time might then come to ease the youngster out with a definite toy, book, or TV suggestion!

Interruptions. If a child is stopped every time, there may be no more interruptions—and perhaps no more conversation either. When to overlook, when to mention the discourtesy after the child has his or her say, and when to check quickly all might be used at different times. (There is another important point to think about: How often do *we* interrupt—or apologize for doing so? How well do we wait for "our turn"?)

The original question was: Are manners important? They are all tied up with getting along with, understanding, having respect for, liking and being liked by other people. We can be definite about such factors—all of them are very important! So what have you done today to help your young child reach those goals—through the example you set or the guidance and careful correction you provide? And have you kept in mind that a preschooler usually isn't ready for "grown-up manners"?

Thumbs, Nails, Noses—and Young Children

The behavior of young children can be changed. Some of it that you don't like and find difficult to live with will be out-grown. However, you may be making a serious mistake if you just sit around and wait for bad habits to disappear. Time will not take care of all of them. Ask yourself: *What does my child do that I want to change? What behavior needs improving?*

Start by listing what your youngster does that you feel is wrong or bad. It will probably help if your husband or wife agrees with you so that you can work together. Keep in mind that an orderly plan usually is better than nagging, screaming, and hitting. Affection and praise pay off, too. The fable about the tough wind and the soothing sun fits this situation. Do you remember how much more the calm, gentle sun was able to accomplish?

Parents of young children often worry about these three kinds of behavior: *thumb-sucking, nail-biting,* and *nose-picking.* All of them can be eliminated for most children—but it takes time, patience, a planned approach, your own self-control, and love.

Thumb-sucking. Babies suck their fingers because it is natural for them to do. A bottle, a pacifier, or nursing is a substitute in infancy, but what should you do about it when your child is two...or three...or four. Pulling a finger from a child's mouth or slapping hands will seldom eliminate the habit. Some people use gloves or bad-tasting materials on a child's fingers. They might work, but there may be a better way.

Enjoyable toys or games that keep a child occupied, a snack at the right time, or just waiting patiently until the need no longer exists may solve the problem. So often children suck their thumbs because there is nothing else to do. So read a book together, go for a walk, or turn on a TV program you carefully select. Any of those activities can be a lot more satisfying to a young child than staring into space and sucking a finger.

Nail-biting. As with many other habits of children, you might ask, "What is the reason?" Behavior is caused by something, the psychologists say. Is there too much pressure or tension because of a family situation? (Adults sometimes bite their fingernails for similar reasons, by the way.) Do you expect too much for your child's age, development, or intelligence? It isn't easy to correct all the situations that can result in nail-biting, but some can be eliminated. You can also concentrate (but not too much) on the nails themselves. A compliment when they *are* clean (or when even one of them is clean or a little longer than the rest!) and a word of praise for clean hands may help begin to turn off the habit.

Nose-picking. Many of the same causes of nail-biting are behind this one. Even more parental anger may be aroused because this habit is often unpleasant to see. Keeping a child busy with an enjoyable can occupy hands in ways you can accept better.

Many parents have succeeded in eliminating these three habits as well as others they don't like. Certain rules will help:

- The less attention you give to them the easier it might be to correct them.
- Noticing small improvements and quick reactions to them may pay off. Kind words, a smile, or a hug are often the best rewards, usually more successful than humiliation or anger.
- "If you do that, this will happen." Be as honest as possible in mentioning the bad effects of unwanted behavior…like people don't enjoy watching it.
- A parent's own cleanliness, orderliness, and good habits can set a pattern for the children. Our children copy us—and that may sometimes be an unhappy thought!

Researchers use words like "behavior modification" and "reinforcement." The fancy language doesn't hide their objective, which is similar to ours: reduce or eliminate questionable behavior, increase what is acceptable, and make our children's lives and ours more pleasant.

Spoiled? Pampered? Not my Child!

Do you have a school-age child on whose teeth-brushing, hand-washing, and shower-taking you check? Do you have a teenager for whom you still wait up late at night? Parents of young children should take a hint. The need for all of that checking probably began in early childhood.

Your own questions these days may be simple to ask, but a little uncomfortable to answer: Do you give your child toys, games, or other gifts that he doesn't need and may not even want? Or another question: Do you do things for her when help is no longer necessary? Maybe it will be done clumsily, not as well as you would do it, but well enough for a small child. After all, you've had a lot more practice tying shoelaces, brushing teeth, and feeding yourself.

A smart man wrote many years ago that parents could have a serious problem if they weren't careful. Alfred Adler, an Austrian psychiatrist, warned that pampering might become the basic relationship between parents and children, and he may have been right. Not all parents give presents instead of a few minutes of their own time, but it is sometimes easier. If we work all day, we're tired. If we are single parents, we may want to "make up" for the missing parent. If there are too many questions, who has the patience to answer all of them? So when we give a "thing" rather than "ourselves" or when we do too much for a child instead of gradually fading from the picture (as he grabs for a shoelace, zipper, toothbrush, or spoon, for example), we may be creating a problem we don't expect. "Gimme," "Do it for me," or "What's in it for me?" can become part of a child's daily life.

It doesn't end in early childhood either. In school such children might become underachievers because no one pays them off with rewards fast enough. They may insist on being the center of attention or "I won't play...I'll sulk." Bragging or using hair or clothes to grab the limelight may be the result of earlier smothering. Anger, hostility, selfishness, and bitter competition sometime follow the child who wants her own way and for whom parents do more than they should in the early years.

Dressing and feeding an infant is all right, but it's not all right for the five-year-old. Two-year-olds can often point to and name objects in a picture book, so we don't have to do it for them. Three-year-olds might be able to use the bathroom alone; they may not always be tidy, but a good rule to follow sometimes is: "Expect and you will get." Most four-year-olds prefer sand, water, mud, and make-believe friends rather than fancy, expensive toys. Five-year-olds may need reminding about washing up before meals, but they don't need help doing it most of the time. If we know what to expect at each age, taking our hint from what a young child says and does, we won't become a pampering parent.

A good nursery school teacher practices the rules of helping when needed, of smiles, nice words, and a hug when earned, and of a gentle but firm refusal to do what the child can do alone. Watching that kind of a person in action can teach parents a trick or two. (After all, we don't become an instant success at parenthood just because we had a baby! It's a tough job for which few of us had any preparation.)

Pampering can result in a child's laziness or a later the-world-owes-me-a-living attitude. But sometimes it is necessary. A skinned knee, no invitation to a friend's birthday party, or a complicated puzzle all require our time and understanding. It takes parental wisdom to see how thin the line is between the need for helping out and keeping hands off.

It's nice to be wanted and besides, we enjoy it. But there's danger in being too available. The trouble is that we sometimes don't find out until it may be too late.

Telling the Truth—It isn't Easy!

"It's *my* toy!"

"Yes, I *did* wash my hands."

"I just took *two* cookies."

"There was this big man—and he came in my room when you put out the light—and he grabbed me—and…"

It isn't easy to tell the truth all the time, especially when you are two, three, four, or five years old. But when a young child does *not* tell the truth, is the child lying on purpose? Or are there other reasons for the wrong words to come out?

"*My* toy" is often said because the child wants it so much, even though it is really understood that it belongs to someone else. Little ones know that parents want to hear that their children are clean, so it's easier to say that they *did* wash their hands. Isn't that a lot better than explaining that the water was too hot, the faucet too tight, or the task done well would have meant being away from all the fun too long? Mama may be angry if I took more than *two* cookies—so that's a good number to tell her. And it may be fun to imagine or to fool people about that big man in the dark. Besides, that story might help keep Mom or Dad in the dark room with me.

Telling the truth doesn't come naturally. It has to be learned, and that takes time. It is so easy not to tell the truth, to *avoid punishment* ("No, I didn't cross the street"), *get parents' approval* ("yes, I picked up all the toys"), *feel older* ("I can too go down that slide"), *escape blame* ("baby sister spilled the milk"), or *create excitement* ("their house fell right down").

Because children sometimes don't know all the right words to use, or haven't yet learned differences in sizes, shapes, or directions, they may stretch the truth—like "I saw lots and lots of fire engines" (although maybe there were only two), or "His daddy has the biggest car in the world."

Everyone needs recognition and affection, and children may lie for them. After all, what's so serious about saying that I did what you wanted and then you'll give me a smile or a kiss? It may also seem to be worth a little lie to see how surprised people look or to get a father who seldom visits to stay longer. A young child doesn't often think ahead to the fact that you may find out the truth. Young children can't always tell the difference between "real" and "pretend," or between make-believe for fun and telling a lie to get something they want. So what can you do about it? Here are some practical hints:

- Recognize that lies are part of every young child's life.
- Try not to use the word "lie" or to call a child a "liar" when you are not getting the whole truth. If the child thinks you have a low opinion of him, his main reason to try better may be destroyed.
- Understand that a child is less likely to lie again if she knows you aren't fooled, that you don't like it when she lies ("although I never stop loving you"), and that her lies upset her friends.
- Explain that "make-believe" and "really true" aren't the same. Age two is too early to try to explain, but by three or four it may be easy.
- Say, "Tell me what you really saw (or took or did)" rather than "Don't you dare lie to me!" Severe punishment sometimes leads to children becoming more skillful at lying instead of being more truthful.
- Prevent situations that encourage lies. It doesn't help to ask whether hands were washed when you can see how dirty they still are. If you ask, you might have two problems—carelessness and lying. So don't ask; tell or take instead.
- Recognize that a child who *always* seems to lie or make believe may need professional help. But a little bit of it is completely normal.
- Set the example yourself. It's probably your own business when you boast about cheating in work or play or lie about age—but do your young children have to hear you? If you can't avoid the original act, perhaps you can at least stop talking about it. Lying is kind of contagious, and young children learn from what they see adults do.
- Break promises or give dishonest answers—but recognize that's a form of lying, too.

Accidents, Safety, and Young Children

Each year 15,000 children die in accidents and 700,000 are hurt by toys. One out of every five is injured, maybe even crippled for life. Will your youngster be one of them this year? Most accidents—and the pain and tears they cause—can be avoided.

Toys. Parents sometimes forget the main rules of toy safety: almost any toy can be unsafe if a child is too young for it or doesn't know how to use it; all toys should be checked for loose, broken, missing, and rusty parts; toys not put away might be tripped on—and it isn't only children who fall over them! Button eyes on dolls, tiny wheels, and other small parts too often end up in throats, ears, and noses. Just as dangerous can be the wires, pins, and tacks that sometimes stick out of stuffed animals, pointed pieces of wood that have lost their rubber suction cups, and sharp edges of plastic and metal. Plastic wrappings and caps and guns that make too much noise can also create problems.

Most toys seem so harmless. But colorful rattles can break, and the bright balls inside might look good enough to eat. Chemical sets and toys for big children may get into small hands and rubbed into tired eyes.

Automobiles. Adult supervision is the best prevention, but so is quietly telling a child what to do and not to do, repeated again and again. Knowing "red" and "green" and looking both ways are still very important. A car seat that is too big or too small, seat belts not used, and small children standing up in a moving automobile, or with arms or head outside the window, could mean trouble. So can careless backing up in the driveway. It may lead to the scream of a hurt child, too small to be seen even if the rear-view mirror is used. A tricycle in traffic, a ball bouncing into the street, and thoughtless running between parked cars might all result in injury.

Medicines. High up and hidden away is the rule to follow. It's dangerous to say, "It tastes just like candy" because small children may then think it's all right to take a lot of it. Problems can be created by adult carelessness: not reading labels; not emptying old bottles before putting them in the trash; giving medicine in the dark from the wrong bottle. If you want to avoid danger for your young child, think about these, too:

- Playground equipment—sharp edges, bolts that stick out, and no adults to watch
- Sharp objects—pencils, tools, ice picks, scissors, knives, without an adult to show how and when to use them
- Small objects—thumb tacks and marbles to swallow, and keys to put into open electrical wall outlets
- Tricycles—two or more riding at a time
- Household supplies—bleaches, garden spray, kerosene, insect powders, ammonia, and moth balls not well enough hidden
- Stoves—with pot handles within easy reach
- Stairways without protective gates, patio doors without warning marks on the glass, loaded guns, window screens rusted or not fastened, bath time with no supervision, old refrigerators and toy boxes with large doors, clothes lines hanging too low—and the problems that fire and water can cause
- Just two more items for you to check: Do you have a first aid kit? Do you know how and when to use what's in it?

Perhaps most important of all is the way you act—for example, with tools, matches and other possibly dangerous items. You may want your child to be safe but not scared, careful but not timid, and have fun while playing, skating, swimming, and climbing a tree. If you know the rules of accident prevention and safety, that's fine. A lot of parents do—but they sometimes need to be reminded.

Toilet Training: The Greatest Problem of Early Childhood?

Ask most parents of young children, and they'll tell you: "If I can only get my child toilet trained! It will all be easy from that time on." What parents usually want to know is how and when to get the job done. So here are some hints.

- Starting either too early (under 1 year) or too late (around 3) can be a mistake. For most children, from 1½ to 2 years of age seems to be the best time to begin.
- By 2 to 3½ years most children have both the needed understanding and control. (But some take more, some less time.)
- Even then accidents occur due to illness, jealousy of a new baby, playing outside, being away from home, or other causes.
- All children are on different time schedules, and when they start has little to do with their intelligence.
- Parent attitudes are very important. Scolding, spanking, shaming, or showing disgust may lead to a poor parent-child relationship. Far more suitable are these: Showing interest ("I'll help you"); providing encouragement or praise ("What a good boy/girl you are"); being gentler, accepting, patient, and consistent.
- Young children usually want to be clean and to please their parents, but they can't do either until they are mature enough.
- All girls do not start before all boys. There are slow ones and fast ones in both sexes.
- Try to control your enthusiasm over toilet successes. Sound eating, sleeping, and dressing habits are also important, but we usually don't go

wild with compliments when they are acquired. All are natural parts of a child's development.

Some parents recognize that their young children, even before age one, are on a regular bowel schedule. If they take them quickly enough, the diaper may stay clean. However, this does not represent a lasting toilet habit, which is there only when a child knows what to do and is able to do it.

Between one and a half to two years (or a little earlier or later) you'll notice the warning signs of a coming bowel movement—a sudden stop in play activity, a red face, a straining noise, how the child stands, or even a plea for help. That's the time for a calm, quiet trip to the bathroom. Sometimes you'll be too late, of course. But it is a sign of progress if your child tells you even after it's happened. The child deserves praise anyway. "Next time try to tell me more quickly, honey."

If you want to use a "potty chair," choose one that sets on the bathroom floor and which a child can use without help. It's not a toy, though; it has only one use. If nothing happens when the child tries to use it, it may be just too early. Forcing a child to sit there for too long may actually be cruel.

Even before control is total, you might try using training pants. Their use indicates that you have faith in the child and that the youngster is growing up. Even if there is an occasional accident, use praise when all goes well—or nearly well. It takes time to learn how to take clothing down or up, to learn to flush the toilet, to use toilet paper correctly, to wash and dry hands—and it takes explanation and also "showing how."

It isn't easy for parents to be or act relaxed during this important learning period. We all know that. But many of us also know that the more nervous and worried we are—and show our child that we are—the more concerned the child will be. So maybe if there is a problem, we as parents "own" it. Young children learn (rather than are "trained") to do something about it. And they do—in time! Two brief additional items:

- Neither parent has total responsibility for these activities. Both are—or should be—involved.
- The words you use to describe aspects of the toilet training situation are your choice—whatever you are comfortable with and whatever words you want your child to use.

Good luck!

Enuresis—A Fancy
Word for Wetting

Let's face it: One of the most difficult problems of early childhood is bed-wetting—or wetting during the day. It is even worse with an older child, but that isn't our concern here. The correct word for it is *enuresis* (urinating when one doesn't want to). And that's a point to understand right at the start: No child enjoys being wet. It's uncomfortable. It sometimes causes mothers and fathers to yell, even at each other. It may result in punishment.

Although urinating schedules differ from child to child, certain age patterns are fairly "normal":

- Before 1½—little regular control, unless your youngster is both bright and physically mature—or you're lucky!
- Between 18 months and 2 years—some sign (facial or gesture), especially if you have "caught" him or her regularly.
- 2 to 3 years old—firm beginnings and pride in control— longer time between bathroom visits—may tell you ahead of time, or try to "go" alone (not always a success!).
- 3 to 4 years old—often dry all night, awakens and asks to be taken.
- After 4—becomes a private, routine affair, but even at 5 a child may need reminding or have accidents due to excitement, an upsetting situation at home or school, or play that is too much fun to leave even for a few minutes.

Not all children stay dry by the same age. Only about half of them make it by two and half years old, and girls are often faster than boys. The standing up and sitting down routine by sexes is learned by what they observe or hear from you in simple terms.

In addition to not being "ready" yet, there are other causes for enuresis—tensions due to family turmoil (arguments, separations, divorce); a new house or location; a new baby; parent pressure or anger; adjusting to preschool or kindergarten; illness. Delayed training may even be hereditary. How was it with your older children, or with you or your wife or husband? Sometimes there are reasons like a strange bathroom away from home or the fright of a loud toilet, getting adult attention or "getting even" for being punished, or the fact that a child is high-strung, easily excited, or very cold.

So what can you do about it? First, try to discover the cause for the problem. There usually is a reason which you can eliminate or reduce. If your child is ordinarily happy and active, enuresis will often stop when the tense or unusual situation passes. Perhaps the objective opinion of a good preschool teacher can help you. And if your youngster is five or six, and you really have no idea at all why this is happening, it may be time for a physical check-up and a conversation with your doctor about emotional problems. The experts on this subject don't agree on solutions. Among their ideas are the following:

- *A regular schedule.* Before and after mealtime, nap time and bedtime, and whenever your child is dry for a few hours—this routine may gradually adjust to the child's own needs and habits.
- *Your matter-of-fact attitude.* Excessive praise or repeated concern may delay the process.
- *Consistent verbal instructions* ("let's go to the bathroom"), *gestures* (pointing toward it), and *manual guidance* (physically taking the child there). Alone or in combination, these can lead toward routine follow-up by your youngster.
- *Rewards for dryness.* Small toys and calm, complimentary words or smiles often help. Once the habit is established, rewards can be removed or "faded out."
- *Mechanical devices.* Loud signals that start as soon as wetting does have been effective, but less so with young children. More normal methods based on a patient, orderly approach should be tried first.

Other suggestions include waking the child during sleeping hours (may result in a dry bed, but not necessarily training that lasts), reducing evening fluids, expanding the child's bladder capacity (with a physician's advice), and involving your youngster in changing pajamas and sheets.

Some parents try too early and too hard. Others think yelling will help. It won't, nor will punishment and shame. In fact, they may even cause delay and tension. And don't expect success all at once or judge by other children in your or other families. Good luck!

Helping Your Child Grow Up

Have Fun with Food

"Three things, among many, are important to young children," a well-known pediatrician recently said. "*Diet, exercise,* and *tension*… And of course, they are important to their parents, too." This book discusses all of them, but now we will focus on the first one—diet—in a different way.

All living things need good food. That point is easy to get across to young children through the skinny, lost puppy that is so weak, the goldfish that died because it wasn't fed, and the grass that needs water and fertilizer to be green.

Little children sometimes have strange ideas about food, like…orange juice, milk, and eggs come only from cartons…apples and peaches start out in a supermarket bin…all bananas are yellow (although one study which asked a group of poor children to draw a picture of them resulted in bunches of brown bananas). We should not be surprised if a young child expects all cheese to be in slices, bread in cellophane, chicken in parts, and butter in packages. After all, that may be the only way the child has seen them.

We can, of course, *tell* them the facts. Some fruits grow on trees, and milk comes from cows. However, they can pick up the ideas better if they *see* what we tell them about. A few hours of learning squeezed into your busy schedule may help. The fun is that you too may find out something you didn't know and perhaps will even enjoy the whole experience. Here are five ideas to consider. How about trying one or two of them this weekend?

- Take your youngster to the supermarket and talk about what you buy, how you select the lettuce, and why you choose that can of tuna. There is a good reason for every selection. Share it freely once in a while.
- Visit a bakery together and ask to go in back. Sometime arrange your visit for when they are baking (although usually that is too early in the morning for most of us).

- Make a big thing out of going where foods start. A dairy farm, a ranch, corn or wheat in cultivation, or trees with real fruit on them (and the excitement for little fingers to pick, wash, and eat what they themselves select)—these may all be only an hour or two away. It's just that somebody has to be thoughtful enough to plan the trip and realize that it may be worth using expensive gasoline to see those eyes open wide in surprise and pleasure.
- Go to specialty shops. Taste the cheese samples, and see it in big wheels. Learn together what the Italian, Greek, Chinese, and other groceries sell, how their products are used, what they cost, and how they taste. See whole chickens and fresh-caught fish, not just frozen pieces.
- Plan your menus (with their help) around what you have bought together. Combine and flavor foods for soups, or salads, again with their help. How far you carry their cooperation (and messiness!) into your cooking depends on your patience, of course. When you find your anger and voice rising it is time to stop! Making ice cream, cakes, and frosting (with the happy lick of the spoon at the end) may be for only the strongest parents.

A few related thoughts for you: 1) Don't include a trip to a slaughterhouse. Neither your stomach nor theirs may be able to take it. 2) Use these experiences also to help teach about money. It's not too early to discuss what food and other purchases cost. 3) Suggest that your youngster's preschool director provide fresh fruits and vegetables at their next parent open house. They are so much better than the sugared-punch-chocolate-mix routine.

The U.S. Department of Agriculture believes in this common sense approach to foods. "The most crucial influence of nutrition on potential mental development is from three months before birth to about three years of age," they say. Ten million children live in poverty; "many of these children, *plus many others from nonpoor families,* were inadequately nourished." With a few of the simple ideas suggested above you can help your young children learn about foods and how they relate to his or her good health.

The Young Child's Eating and Meals
(Pleasure or Problem?)

You are what you eat, say some people. And the adult your child will become depends to an important degree on what he eats in his youngest years. Many of us fight our adult battle of overweight and high cholesterol, wrong foods, overeating, and poor meal schedules. However, there are some easy ways to help your young child get off to a better start.

- Recognize that the amount a child should eat depends on his appetite, size, and tendency to put on weight. Although you should choose what he eats, let him decide on how much.
- Understand that each child has food likes and dislikes just as adults do. Why not try to appeal to her tastes? Supermarket and grocery store shelves provide a lot of variety these days.
- Provide between-meal snacks, but they needn't be candy, sweet cookies, potato chips, and soft drinks. A regular snack time based on milk, fruit juice, raw vegetables, dry cereals, and dry or fresh fruit is healthful— and most children like them.
- Encourage your child to eat what is "good for him" through small servings, mild seasoning, separate foods (most youngsters don't like casseroles, and they do like divided plates), colorful foods (like gelatins and pieces of parsley), and various textures (chewy, crisp, and soft, rather than all the same).
- Make it easy for her little fingers and hands. Soup in a cup, small bite-size pieces, and food that can be picked up often help cut down on mealtime nagging, yelling, and jangled nerves. (By the way, so can plastic dishes, washable floor coverings, and chairs to match children's sizes.)

- Try to schedule meals that don't last too long and at times when young-sters are rested. That may help reduce the tension many of us face after a tough day's work, fighting traffic, or figuring out how to pay the expanding family bills. We need a calm mealtime as much as children do—perhaps more!

Preschoolers often go through stages of wanting to dictate what, where, and when they will eat. That's normal. Maybe eating alone or earlier will help solve that problem. No member of the family really has the right to spoil it for everyone else.

Including all the main elements in the daily diet is less difficult than it may seem at first. It used to be rigidly recommended that so much milk, fruit, vegetables, meat, bread, and cereals were needed every day, but now the recommendation is simpler. A child from two to five years old needs 25 to 30 grams of protein and 1,250 to 1,600 calories a day. Here are some sample protein and calorie figures:

Food	Protein (grams)	Calories
one glass of whole milk	9	160
one egg	6	80
one ounce of meat	7	80
one ounce of cheese	7	105
a dish of ice cream	2	95
a raw carrot	1	20
mashed potatoes	2	93
a banana	1	100

Giving a child too much protein is costly and nutritionally wasteful. It is better to fill the rest of his diet with foods he likes that are light in both protein and fats.

Now, a rather touchy point. Our children learn a great deal from us, and if we are the chocolate, chewing gum, popcorn, rich ice cream type, why should we expect them to be different? If we steadily nibble sweets and have an irregular meal schedule, why be surprised if they do, too? If we enjoy foods that are fried or heavy in fats, perhaps we should cut down a bit, for the sake of our own heart as well as for our children's health. After all, we are the most important teacher they will ever have by the example we set every day.

The Teeth of Young Children

Half of all two-year-olds have some dental decay…two of three five-year-olds who go to dentists have cavities…one of every ten has eight or more cavities. More than nine of ten six-year-olds surveyed in one state had tooth decay. You may think: Those facts don't refer to my young child—or "baby teeth" fall out anyway, so who cares?

Just because they are all gone in a few years doesn't mean they are of no importance. They are. Healthy first teeth hold a space for the later permanent ones, provide proper chewing to help assure nourishment, and contribute to good speech and to correct development of your child's jaws and face. If neglected, the result might be infection, pain, and sleepless nights for you and your youngster.

Most experts agree that children should have their first visit to the dentist by the time they are two or three, and then twice a year. Your attitude in connection with that visit is very important. To say that the dentist won't hurt the child may bring up a thought that never even occurred to your youngster. If the visit is combined with something enjoyable (a trip downtown or an hour together in the park or playground), it might become an enjoyable experience for both of you.

In addition to regular dental examinations and care, there are four other steps toward sound teeth for your young child.

Diet. Sugar, candy, soft drinks, and sweet snacks (especially ones that can stick to teeth) are the enemy. Rewarding a child with a candy bar does him no favor, especially between meals when the candy has a lot of time to attack the tooth enamel. Natural and refined sugar are both bad.

A sound diet is good for teeth, as well as for general health, so think about fruit and vegetables, bread and cereals, milk and dairy products, and meat or other protein foods. Too many soft foods aren't recommended; chewing helps clean off the teeth and makes gums healthy.

Brushing. At two (or even earlier) your child often wants to copy you, so let her try—with your help. Brush after every meal if possible. Removing food is important, but even more valuable is removing *plaque*, a sticky film of bacteria that can destroy teeth. Several ways to brush help get the job done. Here's one you might consider: Bristles angled toward the gums; short, easy strokes on all surfaces (outer, inner, biting); narrow front end of brush to get inside front teeth, top and bottom. The brush itself should be soft and small, with a flat brushing surface—and replace it when the bristles become frayed or bent.

Dental floss can remove plaque that a brush may not reach, but carefully supervise its use. After all, those are tender young gums! If you tie the ends together, making a ten to twelve inch circle, it will be easier to use.

How well is the plaque removed? A liquid or tablet made with harmless red food dye can tell you; if color sticks to teeth, more brushing is needed.

Fluoride. People still argue about it, but most dentists and health professionals agree that fluoride strengthens the enamel and reduces decay. Numerous studies show that children who drink fluoridated water from birth have up to 65 percent less tooth decay. Fluoride in the water, an application of it to child's teeth by a dentist or in the toothpaste, or tablets prescribed by a dentist or physician are ways to use this element.

Your own example. Whether you brush your teeth often and well, use dental floss, visit the dentist regularly, and control your diet are all watched closely by those little eyes. Young children look and learn—and you are the one they see as a model. Dental decay is our most common disease. It affects 98 percent of us. But here's a happier thought: Through *dental care, proper diet, brushing, fluoride,* and *example,* dental decay can be controlled in young children.

Television—Good or Bad for Young Children?

"Television viewing for the child under five should be wisely selected, seen by child and parent, and followed by a short, fun discussion of what they saw."—Miss Frances, Ding Dong School

You should be involved right from the beginning with your young children in their television watching, says this expert. Ask yourself: How often do you look at a program all the way through with your youngster? How often do you talk together about one? In many homes television fits into a different kind of pattern. The set is sometimes turned on early in the day and kept on whether anyone is watching or not. Or, there may be two sets on at the same time in different parts of the house.

Television isn't bad. The main problem is that it is often used badly. In some families it is a young child's only activity. Some parents like it because it might keep children out of mischief, and there is no mess to pick up or to trip over, no toys, clay, water, blocks, or beads. For both learning and entertainment, do you know of anything else that costs so little and is always there ready for use? But just as it is with other parts of our lives—the family automobile, movies, and meals, for example—it has to be planned for and used well. Here are some suggestions for you to think about:

- Help choose the programs your preschool child watches. It takes only a little time. You have to watch them yourself once in a while.
- Select programs that are fun as well as those that can teach your child. Some, of course, can both entertain and teach. You don't watch only educational adult programs, do you? You enjoy the ones you see, and so should your youngster. "The days that make us happy make us wise,"

said another expert in this field, and he meant that we—and our young children—can learn best if what we watch or do is also enjoyable.

- Talk about the program with your children, both before and after. "What was it about?" "Why did the people do certain things?" "Which persons did you like—or dislike?" Keep your discussion short. A few minutes are enough. Let it be fun for both of you.
- Limit their TV watching. That suggestion means nothing unless the other hours are enjoyable, too. A good preschool, day care center, or nursery school should be among your other first choices. Playing with neighbors' children and sharing a little of your time are other possibilities. The problem with TV isn't so much what it does, but what it might prevent, like conversation, games, play with toys—and time with you. The television story may be good, but not as good as the one you make up with your child as the main character.
- Control your own watching of television. Parents are a young child's main teachers. If you turn on the set the minute you get home and leave it on through the late, late show, what can you expect? But if you select the programs you want and have a little peace and quiet around the house the rest of the time, your example can be a good one to follow.

Cartoons can be either good or bad. Popeye and his spinach still provide a useful bit of advice, and squashed insects and other animals come right back to life.

Violence on TV is something for you to watch out for. One study of nursery school children said that they imitated what they saw. Fighting, killing, and torture can wait until your young child is old enough to take them in stride. Middle-of-the-night tears and screaming can sometimes be traced directly to TV programs that are not suitable.

Watching television together can be boring unless you both enjoy it. Laughing at it, side by side, can be great. Try it out on this afternoon's or early evening's cartoons as a starter. Also do it on parts of *The Wizard of Oz* the next time it is shown.

In summary: Select, control, and use television with your young child. It has a lot to offer.

Money. . .Money. . .Money

Many of us spend more time on earning money and how to use it than we do on anything else. However, few of us think much about it in connection with our young children. But we should, from two points of view—ours and theirs.

Our income has to take care of all the everyday family needs, of course. Food, health, clothing, and home expenses must be covered, but then what? Vacations and travel? Insurance? Movies and restaurants? No matter what other uses for money are important to you, the cost of your preschool child's basic start in life should be high on your list.

A good early childhood education program can pay off in many ways. For example, few parents can supply the professional supervision available in a well-developed preschool. Nor can they usually provide broad communication, behavior, physical, number, and prereading skills—or safe, large, and varied equipment and materials. You certainly may do a great deal at home, but a sound preschool can expand your young child's environment and help him or her do well when the later school program starts. So when you decide how to spend your money, your youngster's early education ought to be right up there after the basic necessities of family life—or perhaps even among them, according to some authorities on child development.

Another important point of view toward money is how young children look at it. Their attitudes begin much earlier than you may think. They hear and watch what you say and do about it. They like the shape of coins, the pleasant feel, the shiny look, and the jingling noise. By three, they know it can buy things—"good" ones like candy, ice cream, and toys, and others like food and clothing. They have usually learned that it's not to be put into their mouths or to be played with. They also may know that some children are "rich" and others "poor," although they might be a little mixed up on that point as one of the Rockefeller children who received only a few cents for allowance every week.

Among the ways you can help a preschool child learn to handle money are these:

- Provide a small allowance every week. Give it regularly, not for good behavior and not taken away for bad behavior. The size? Your decision, but 10¢ to 25¢ may be enough.
- Talk about how Daddy and Mommy earn money. If possible, have the child visit you at work.
- Let him make simple buying decisions that are important to him—a choice of a toy car or an ice cream cone, for example.
- Take her to the bank with you and explain very simply what you do there.
- Protect the child from worry about money crises. Nothing is gained by sharing them with a young child, and much can be lost, like the child's security and faith in you.
- Let your child make small purchases and return with the change, but not handle amounts of money that would upset you if they are lost.
- Encourage saving in a play bank at home, using coins that relatives might provide. Some of the allowance may be saved, of course, but the rest is for spending—wisely.
- Include your child in simple discussions about not-too-long-range family decisions, like saving for or buying a TV set.
- Help him divide a pile of pennies for presents at Christmas time, and let him share the fun of selecting and buying gifts.

Preschool children are too young to earn money for work done at home and should not receive pay for doing regular household jobs. Taking out the garbage, helping with the dishes, and picking up after the dog shouldn't be paid for any more than taking a bath or tying shoelaces.

Teaching a young child about money isn't easy. But we should begin early to help prepare them for how hard it is to earn and to use money well. Only by having and spending money (with your guidance) can a young child learn the differences among coins and what should and should not be done with them and other money.

Independence—
Your Child Needs It

"Do it my own self...Let me do it...Yes, I can...Don't hold me so tight." The second a baby is born, he starts to become an independent person. But it isn't easy. Parents want to hold tightly—and also let go. They may be sorry to see their children grow up, although they often are pleased when they learn to walk, get good school grades, or enter a profession later on. Children want to be free—and still have their parents to depend on. For preschoolers that is especially true when they are tired, sick, or lonely.

If you had to pick the major task of parenthood it might be this: *Help your child become independent and secure. Do it gradually. Be pleased when the child can make decisions without your help.* Years ago there was a play called "The Silver Cord." It was about a mother who controlled and finally destroyed her child. There will always be a place for your suggestions and love, but the "silver cord" has to be loosened and cut. If it isn't, your child might never become an adult able to handle the problems of health, money, getting along with others, and so many more that we all face.

The preschool years are very important for starting your youngster toward independence. It can begin in your own home: Dressing without help (except at first, of course)...playing outside without supervision all the time...picking up and putting away toys, clothes, and groceries...taking messages and running simple errands.

There are many other things you can do in these early years. Let your child be away from you once in a while, at a good day care center or at a neighbor's house...Hold back when you want to help solve a puzzle or problem. Let the child do it...Demand fewer kisses and hugs when the young child goes through a stage of not wanting them...Accept the fact that a young friend may sometimes be wanted more than you are.

How much freedom you give depends on your own background, as well as on your children's desire and ability to do things on their own. They aren't all ready for preschool or staying overnight at a friend's house at the same age, for example. A child's reason for doing things may sometimes be even better than yours. You may have difficulty saying "Yes" when the child wants to stay up a little longer (there may be interesting company in the house), watch the end of a TV show (it may be the best part), or not finish a meal (after all, our tastes for food sometimes differ). If you are rigid, live by strict rules, and insist that the child should, too, your youngster may be afraid to try something new on his own.

Young children need practice and guidance. Instead of having a choice of whether to eat breakfast, they might be permitted to choose this cereal or that one…or this dress or that one rather than a choice from the whole closet. Parents still have to make some decisions for them, of course, like which shoes to wear in the rain and which clothing in the snow.

Children slide back once in a while, as when a new baby comes. The road to independence may have a few bumps in it. Dressing, eating, and bathroom habits, for example, might suddenly seem to go backwards. "Let me help you this time" is then more sensible for you to say than "Aren't you ashamed?" or "You're old enough to know better!" Children like to do things well, but they need:

- Success with loose clothing, large zippers that work, a foot stool or box to help them reach the sink, low clothing hooks, attractive and tasty food, and simple household chores
- Your nice words and smiles when they do tasks well for their age
- Your willingness to let them try, try again, make mistakes, and then succeed

All of that can lead to a child who feels good about what she does, gradually can do more and more on her own, and finally doesn't require a parent's help. We may not like our children to need us so little—but isn't that really the main goal of most thoughtful parents?

A Child's Life is not Perfect

Life can be Tough— Even for Little Children

Even during the most ordinary days and in the most well-adjusted families, young children face problems. They may not seem important to some adults, but after all when you're two, three, four, or five, you haven't yet learned how to solve them. You need help, and you target your parents for assistance. An alert preschool teacher can help, too. To meet these needs of a young child, parents should consider three factors:

- What kinds of *problems* do young children have?
- What *reactions* do they have to their difficulties? What *hints* do they give us?
- What can parents *do* about them?

Problems. In addition to serious ones like a death in the family, getting hurt, and moving away, plus many fears of a little child (like darkness, animals, and loud noises), one of our tasks as parents is to help children adjust to their everyday problems. We may sometimes fail to recognize their problems. They seem so small. A new baby comes to your house...a pet dies...you walk out the preschool door the first few days the child is left there...you and your spouse have an argument...a house down the block catches fire...a friend moves away...a nose is stuffed up, eyes water, a throat is scratchy...the list is almost endless.

Reactions. A lively child may withdraw, suddenly become very quiet. A docile one might strike out, with screams or fists. Smiles turn into tears and silence. You ask what's wrong and receive only a shaking head, a little sob, lips squeezed together in complete silence, or eyes closed and cast down. Because the child can't handle the problem, there may be a tendency to be frightened, even more than the reasons seem to deserve. The words aren't there to explain. But you can tell something is wrong because of the change you so clearly see. Your youngster just isn't acting normally.

What to do. Your awareness that this is a problem comes first. Then your ability to handle it *calmly, patiently,* and *quickly* has to follow. For you merely to ignore the problem, isolate the child, or yell about the tears, screaming, or other difficult behavior doesn't fully control the situation. It may do so temporarily, but a young child treated this way receives little or no help toward solving tough situations now, in the school, and during adult years later on. By what you say and do, you can show that you understand what the child is going through, have gone through it all yourself, and can help solve the problem. It is important to give the impression that you are strong and capable—after all, you really *are*. You have maturity and a long record of solving problems on your side. A few minutes on your lap, a hug, and clean tissue or handkerchief to wipe away the tears may help ease the situation. Then perhaps you can start talking about it.

Just because you handle the matter so calmly doesn't mean you approve of the behavior involved, especially if is almost uncontrollable, violent, or dangerous. You may have to hold or firmly restrain your youngster and put off soothing words and explanations for a while. They can wait until the situation is under better control. There is no reason to rush things before your youngster is ready.

Our task is made so difficult because we were children such a long time ago. It isn't easy to see the world through a child's eyes. But still, we have to try—and to tell ourselves that it is sometimes important to tear ourselves from our own burdens, like money and health problems, and attempt to understand theirs which appear to be so little. Perhaps they are—but not to them.

Do Young Children Worry? Yes!

It is impossible to shelter children from all pain and sorrow. A king once tried. He wanted the young prince's life to be so perfect that he would never face danger, fear, or death. He even had the royal gardeners snip off fading flowers every night while the little prince slept. But in the end, even he found out about sadness and trouble, as we all must. Young children can face them more easily when their parents and preschool teachers use clear and honest words, smiles, and hugs to ease them through difficult times.

The fears of young children can be very real to them. Darkness, loud noises, animals, doctors—the list is long. However, there are ways to prevent them from becoming a habit and to help your youngster be careful without being scared.

Some of the most difficult problems for parents are those related to a broken family and how they affect a young child. Mother, father, and home are his whole world. But neither divorce nor separation will necessarily destroy it.

Little children sometimes worry about matters other than separated or divorced parents and everyday fears like being alone in the dark or getting soap in his or her eyes

- *Moving to a new place.* The problem of leaving somewhere that is familiar can be planned in advance and handled when it happens. It is important to remember that most children (and adults, too) feel better when their own belongings are around them. Having their own toys, books, and other playthings can reduce feelings of loneliness. Most important, of course, is being with their own family, if possible, no matter where they live.

Even small children can understand they have to move if the reason is explained in simple words. "Daddy will look for a job there" or "We will have more money to buy food and other things we need" are ideas that are usually easy to accept.

When parents can adjust to new situations, it is easier for the children to take them in stride. Adult arguments and tears over leaving friends and family too often rub off on the youngsters. You can't (and shouldn't) hide your deep worries about the change, but neither should you let yourself expose them too openly. That's just too much of a burden for a young child to carry.

- *Getting hurt.* When a little child sees a handicapped person, he may think (or say), "Can that happen to me?" At the top of a slide, he might tell you, "No! I'll fall down!" When a little girl becomes aware that she's "made differently" from boys, she may wonder, "What's wrong with me?" Childhood worries like these require honesty and openness. What you say, like "You won't be hurt," "I'll help you," "Let me hold your hand," and "I'll stay here and watch," show that your youngster can depend on you. "Boys and girls are made differently" can help put to rest the idea that something is wrong, missing, or hurt.
- *A death in the family.* What you say about it to a young child is important. How you say it may be even more important. Whispers and secrecy can be a mistake. A young child usually doesn't ask for or need a lot of details. "Why do people die?" (Your answer might refer to "old, "weak," or "his (or her) body wore out.") "Will I die too?" (Everybody does some day, but it will be a long, long time from now.) "What happens to them then?" (Your answer will, of course, depend on your religion. The most honest answer for many of us is, "We really don't know." Telling a young child that "they go to sleep" can be dangerous, possibly creating bedtime fears.)

Keeping the child on a regular schedule (as much as possible) with meal, preschool, TV, and other activities can be helpful when there's a death in the family. If you release your own feelings to a limited extent, children will feel freer about showing theirs. Feelings are easier to talk about when they are in the open. It's also wise to recognize that if boys show concern and sometimes cry, they are taking an important step toward becoming men who are sensitive to the feelings of others, including those of their own wives and children.

"Abuse my Child?
You Hurt my Feelings!"

Have you ever read newspaper headlines like these?

- "Tots locked in car; 2 die at 150°"
- "Child beaten for wetting himself"
- "Young father swings infant; baby brain-damaged"

Of course you have, but it's always about somebody else's family—or at least let's hope it is. Some people think that "child abuse" occurs only when other parents drink or fight or lose their jobs. That's not true. It can certainly happen then, but it can also take place in our own families when—

- A parent's temper runs wild, with screaming, hitting, and no control.
- Parents expect too much, like putting all toys away at two years, toilet training at six months, or feeding himself in infancy.
- A child's looks, intelligence, or physical condition bothers his parents.
- Parents, as children, were abused themselves.
- A family problem causes worry, whether it is based on no job, no money, sickness, death, family split-up, or liquor.

Almost any of us can become a child abuser if the wrong group of problems get together. Reports on nearly 50,000 children hurt by parents came out in just one state in a recent two-year period. Maybe you feel you've seen almost that many cases yourself—like these:

- Grabbing a child by the hand as he reaches for candy in a store; pulling so hard you can almost hear a crack.

- Slapping a youngster so forcefully that he loses his balance and falls against a wall or on the floor.
- Burning a child because the young (or even older) parent doesn't know you should first test the bath water.

Most cases of hurt children happen before they are three or four years old. They may even be unwanted or unloved, a fact that most of us find hard to believe. But what we *can* believe is that children in many families are abused because they mess up a room just cleaned...cry for what seems like no reason...break things...won't go to sleep, or eat, or go to the bathroom as their parents want them to do.

These are the everyday situations against which we have to be on guard and control our tempers. We're bigger, stronger, and older—and we can be dangerous to little children.

Child abuse can also come in other ways. To ignore youngsters, provide a poor diet, insult or ridicule, act sarcastically, or withhold affection can be harmful, too. They need to feel that they can do things well and that some-body respects and loves them. To take away what educators call a worthwhile "self-image" may be cruel treatment that a child can never forget.

A checklist including questions like the five below might help you recognize a problem you had not considered before. You may not have felt this situation could take place in your own family. Even one "Yes" should be a warning.

- Do my temper and self-control get away from me once in a while so that I sometimes really may not know what I'm doing?
- Do I have trouble loving one of my children?
- Do I never seem to have fun with my youngster?
- Do I treat my child as I was treated, striking out, creating pain?
- Do I have problems I can't seem to solve, so I take out my own tears, hurts, and frustrations on a young child?

In many communities help is available when needed: a "hot line" by telephone to an agency like Parents Anonymous, Parental Stress Service, a crisis control center, or one with a similar name; a skilled preschool teacher who will listen and advise or refer; a doctor who knows the harm you can do.

We've made progress in how we treat children. We no longer put little children to work, seldom punish them in ways they don't understand or deserve, and rarely feel they are born "bad." However, their full rights are only now being recognized. We must be aware of the harm we can inflict on our own youngsters. It's sad but true that children sometimes need the greatest protection from the people who say they love them the most.

"Don't be Afraid Little Boy/Girl"
(The fears of young children)

Young children can be afraid of many things:

- Dogs, cats—and some large and little animals that don't even exist
- Dark places and loud noises, voices, and laughter
- Doctors and dentists
- Vacuum cleaners, toilets, fire, and water
- Others you can add

Most of young children's fears are normal and nothing to worry about. They are serious only if they last too long or are too big for the small things that seem to cause them. If a little child is afraid of all animals or cries every time he goes to a preschool, to the bathroom, or has a baby sitter, then perhaps you have a problem. Most children's fears are based on what they have seen or felt, but some they just imagine.

If a child is small, large things may be scary. A slippery tub, his face under water, soap in her eyes, or huge waves might make a child afraid of water. A noise she doesn't understand—like thunder—can bring tears. Being alone in the dark, even in his own room, may cause nightmares.

A wise parent knows how real all of this is to a small child. So you have two goals: Prevent fears from becoming a habit, and help your youngster be careful but not scared. Here are a few examples of how they can be reached:

- *Loud noises.* Say, "Sometimes I still feel funny when it thunders even though I know it won't hurt me. When I was your age, I was scared, too."
- *Darkness.* "I'll stay with you for a while if you want me to. Yes, you can have a small night light if you want one."

- *A large animal.* "Some big dogs jump on people. Let's go up to this one together. We can ask his owner about him."
- *Going down a slide.* "You and I can watch the other children for a while. Then you can decide whether you want to go down."

Holding children's hands and hugging them are important. Give them the feeling that 1) there is nothing to be ashamed of if they are scared, 2) many children and even some adults feel the same way, and 3) "I'm here and I love you."

To tease or laugh at a child because she is afraid could make her hide her fears, which may then be buried deep inside and that's not good. It is just as foolish to tell a child to be "brave," "big," or "strong" when she doesn't feel that way, or to threaten him with dark closets or scary people.

The best approach is to openly discuss what frightens the child. Let him tell you, as many times as he wants to, how it felt to fall down, hear the fire siren close by, or be alone when the lights went out. It often helps to talk things out, just as it does for grown-ups.

You can plan for some fears and avoid them. If you'll be away for a while, talk about it ahead of time. If tonsils are to come out, explain what will happen in words the child can understand. If there will be a new baby, recognize that the child may be worried about someone taking his place. And if bedtime is preceded by a story, a song, or a quiet game, nighttime fears may not occur.

A child who is frightened once shouldn't be exposed to the same scare soon again. You can't throw her into deep water and expect her to laugh the next time you try it! One who isn't ready to jump off a wall or fence shouldn't have to jump. If he does, he may be even more scared the next time. When he understands something, he might more easily accept it. Let him push the little switch that turns on the vacuum cleaner—and be there to smile and hold him.

Your own calmness, willingness to listen and explain, and patience even when the fears seem silly to you will help your child overcome them. All fears and dangers can't be prevented, but you can make them less serious. A happy child is one who can take them in stride.

"Nobody Knows my Name"
(The mobile child)

What do rich and poor young children have in common? A lot of things, we hope, including good health and a happy home. Two additional factors they may share are anxiety and loneliness—if the rich ones are in families that move often, chasing the dollar up the business or professional ladder, and the poor ones belong to migrant families that follow the crops.

Much written about "the mobile family" tells the story of migrant workers and their children. But they're only one part of a much larger group. Many parents do not raise their children where they themselves grew up. Daddy has a new job, the military travel orders came through, let's follow the sun and leave snow and sleet behind, rural-to-city and city-to-suburb, death of a parent or divorce—and here we go again with a new home, new environment, and new problems.

Children—even the little ones—may worry about and perhaps even resent the move. To us it may be no big thing. After all, we may have done it before. But to them it is a removal from much that is familiar, and there is little in their experience to tell them that all will turn out fine. Certain facts about children of mobile families are worth considering.

- They vary as much in their ability to adjust to a new setting as they do in their height, weight, and looks. Some can easily cope with the change. Others become frustrated and apathetic, sometimes even angry toward those who seem to have a steadier, more secure family life.
- Preschool and school handicaps are less likely to occur when the move is during the summer and if the changes don't take place too frequently (some children move 10-12 times during their preschool and elementary school years).

- Family mobility is usually hardest on preschool children and teenagers. The former need order and continuity, and adolescents sometimes seem to be upset by even slight irregularities, let alone a 2,000 mile move.
- The total adjustment is often easier for the child with above-average ability than it is for the so-called average or slower youngster. Their numerous interests frequently ease the transition of more able children.

Parents can help their youngsters adjust to a new home and location. Full sharing of their own stress and insecurity (if they *are* really sad, resentful, or insecure because of the move) may not be appropriate, not with little children anyway. But it sometimes helps to admit (at least to ourselves) that we're all in this together, we'll all have some adjustments to make, and we'll come through it all right. Besides, a move sometimes has the important side-effect of pulling the family together.

The family-on-the-move has a lot of company. Most of us are caught up in the search for greener pastures, leaving the extended family and familiar places behind. Our preschool children are sometimes ignored in that whole process. "After all, aren't they too small to be affected by such changes?" Watch their faces and listen to what they say. You'll find out that they also need a sense of security. Just by being there with a toy, a book, a laugh, or a trip to the grocery store or a TV program watched together, you can help the lonely moment pass. If only it could be eliminated so quickly for adults!

Preschool teachers can also be helpful. It won't hurt the other youngsters at all if the daily routine is interrupted just long enough to welcome the new child with warmth, to select a classmate (preferably one who lives near the newcomer) as a temporary buddy, and to spend a few minutes on "Where are you from?" or "What's it like there?" In sharing such details, a little child seldom continues to feel all alone.

Being lonely isn't pleasant for any of us. The happy part with young children is that such feelings (if they exist at all) seldom last long. With the help of a sensitive parent they may not even occur in the first place.

Traveling with Your Young Children
(Some hints for survival)

Have you ever traveled with young children? Did you know that sometimes it can really be fun? There are two factors that can help you avoid tears, temper tantrums, and tension:

- *Personality—your own.* If it is hard for you to be patient when your youngsters ask for the tenth time, "Are we almost there?" (and you're barely out of the carport), you have these choices: Leave them at home as much as possible—or keep reminding yourself that young children weren't meant to sit still, be quiet, and act polite all the time.
- *Preparation.* Here's where you can show how smart you are. It can make all the difference in travel with their being either miserable or a real pleasure.

Preschool children get restless, so they need *interesting things to do and a variety of items to play with.* They get tired, so they need *rest and occasional stops.* Most travel with young children is by car, and that's fortunate. You can then control the schedule and adjust meal, running-and-jumping, and sleeping time. Remember one important point: All children are different. What satisfies one child may be a complete bore to another. So try to answer this question carefully: What does this youngster like to do at home? These interests won't change the minute the car door shuts, so what was fun at home may also be enjoyable on your trip. Here's a checklist for your "travel survival kit":

- A place in the car that "belongs" to the child
- A toy suitcase or bag for the child (in it can be coloring books, paper,

blunt scissors, crayons, clay, small paper or plastic dolls, and some doll clothing, small cars and trains, cardboard and cut-outs to fold and put together, new and familiar books the child can look at and that you can read together—and a favorite doll or stuffed animal for bedtime)

- Fruit, snacks, salted crackers (said to be helpful for car sickness), cheese, hard-boiled eggs in their shells, a thermos (with milk, fruit juice, or water) and a bag for trash
- A pillow and blanket
- Clothing that doesn't show much dirt or need ironing
- Cleansing and toilet tissues that you can get to quickly
- Plastic tablecloths for picnics and also for bed wetters—and maybe a child-size toilet seat

There are so many things to do in the car: Read. Sing together. Play games; take some and make-up some, like "Who sees…?" based on colors, animals, trees, billboards, or whatever magic in the outside world passes by the car window. Stop at playgrounds and parks once in a while, too.

Be as careful as you can about the food children eat. Salad dressings, puddings, and pastries with moist fillings may be spoiled. Try, as much as possible, to stay with hot foods, fruits you can peel, and the food you take along, rather than overdoing the snack routine.

An early morning start, regular mealtimes, naps and quiet time, stops (to un-cage all of you during the day!), and a stop for the night by late afternoon can round things out—except for one important item: Safety.

You can help make the trip safe if you lock the car doors, don't let children stand on car seats, perhaps put a pad or blanket over the back of the front seat, take a basic medicine kit, and let children run and play only where you can watch them.

It is so nice look forward to something, whether it's ice cream, a picnic, or a swimming pool. But ten minutes to a young child may seem as long as a 12-hour wait for a cup of coffee might be for you!

The car won't always be orderly or serene; don't expect it to be. Be prepared to "roll with" a little turmoil, but planning ahead can cut down on it. Preparing for plane, train, and bus travel will also help. The hints here can be a good starting point in getting ready for it.

You're not the only one sometimes caught in what may seem like a noisy, cluttered human cage on wheels. You have lots of company. Happy traveling!

Playtime and Make-Believe

Seeing Through Children's Eyes

- A child takes a bus trip, and it is exciting and glamorous, even if it is lengthy and overnight. (We take the same one and complain about the facilities on board.)
- A child rides a train and squeals with joy over the motion, noise, and swiftly passing trees, stations, and towns. (We call home and grumble about how dirty it was.)
- The Christmas tree tinsel, a flashing neon sign over a hamburger stand, and a circus, underwater, or animal trick bring a sparkle to a youngster's eyes. (We might think only of how gaudy, cheap, or worn-out it all is.)

The first-time excitement of jumping over a huge ocean wave or taking apart a leaf or acorn is way back in memory for most of us, so far back that it's often forgotten. But that is no reason to blind ourselves to the fact that such childhood thrills come only once, and pass so swiftly. Seeing through the eyes of children is almost impossible. However, it's worth trying. It may even bring a little life to the sameness of our days, a new dimension to a week that stretches ahead looking just like the last one. And there's help available. Great writers can make vivid the feelings many of us forgot long ago, feelings that we should try to recapture at least a bit if we are to have any understanding of our children's dreams, as well as their frustrations.

In *Future Shock* Alvin Toffler notes that if we ask a child to wait two hours for a piece of candy, it is the same as asking his mother to put off having a cup of coffee for 14 hours. Rachel Carson (in *The Sense of Wonder*) says that it may be far more important to share with a young child the thrill of seeing the glistening night lights through a picture window than for the child to go to sleep—and for us to retreat alone to a dark room and a TV screen. In *Dandelion Wine,* Ray Bradbury brings back the excitement of new gym shoes and the sadness of having a friend move away. Glendon Swarthout in *Bless the*

Beasts and Children demonstrates the anguish of youngsters whose parents don't get along well.

Too often we assume that adult problems are overwhelmingly important, and children's problems are insignificant. After all, how can you compare fighting inflation to not being invited to a birthday party? We sometimes overlook one fact—the practice adults have had in coping with all kinds of pressures and disappointments and the fragile defenses of young children. They just can't handle not being chosen to be on the team, for example—not yet anyway.

To get a feel for the roadblocks put in the way of children, join twelve-year-old Jennifer Owsley in *A Handy Guide to Grownups* as she gives us a pre-teen view of parents, teachers, sex, and religion. Or read again, or for the first time, what it is like to be both handicapped and sensitive, like Philip in *Of Human Bondage*, and how he could grow up and be enamored by the coarse Mildred. (Remember Leslie Howard and Bette Davis in those roles?) Or refresh yourself about how it feels to be a child in a small community, through *Our Town, To Kill a Mockingbird,* and *A Death in the Family* (and the play based on it, *All the Way Home*). No, they're not new, but the feelings they expose are far from outdated.

Long ago a story demonstrated how differently a child and adult look at the same event. In *Stella* no one turned up at the party Stella Dallas gave for her daughter. Hardened Stella took it in stride, but her girl received a painful scar. And so did the little boy in Robert Fontaine's *The Happy Time* when he learned the bitter lesson that truth doesn't always pay off.

Make a game of seeing our beautiful world through children's eyes. Try it with flowers, insects, and animals. Get on their level of height and experience. It isn't easy!

Play is Important

With which of these statements do you agree?

- "They're not learning anything. They are only playing."
- "Play is the work and language of children."

If you really believe the first statement, please read on. If you agree with the second, stick with us anyway. What follows will support your point of view.

The importance of play was stressed as long ago as the Bible and as recently as today in every good preschool. An ancient philosopher (Plato) wrote about using apples to teach arithmetic and small tools to help prepare children for adult jobs. A respected educator (Froebel) talked of play and toys to help a child learn and grow. Another (Piaget) connected play with the development of intelligence.

So as parents we ought to respect play...use it...encourage it. It starts in early infancy, with curiosity about the sounds, colors, smells, tastes, and textures of a new world, and continues without interruption through the games and sports of childhood, and on into those of our adult lives. Play also involves toys, being alone or with others, and "enjoying the process and results" of solving problems. "The days that make us happy make us wise" is also true, for children learn through the fun and enjoyment of their home and preschool "work." The problem-solving of making a block tower stay up helps a child cope with other adult problems. A chase game of "It" or "Hide and Seek" can be as serious as your "chase game" of making income cover expenses. Through all the years of *exploring, imitating, trying out,* and *constructing*, a child is preparing to handle the grown-up pressures we all face.

Children's play changes as they mature. When a toy or game becomes too easy, they eagerly take the step up to a harder one. Although individual children vary a great deal, they often go through various stages of play. These are just a few samples:

- At age 2—pushing, pulling, stacking up and knocking down, filling and emptying, opening and shutting...cars, trucks, water play
- At age 3—playing house, hiding games, block building...crayons, paints, wagons
- At age 4—dressing up, pretending, acting out (as firefighters, police officers, doctors, fathers, mothers, for example)
- At age 5—burying treasures, chasing, fantasies (kings, queens, and witches)

What you provide for a child's play needs depends on your awareness of them. They can be met at no or very little cost. This list is as long as your time, patience, and creativity permit... a "housekeeping corner" with pretend clothes...a cardboard frame around a piece of old sheet and a light behind it (to create a "shadow stage")...colorful pictures from old magazines...clay, dolls, books, songs, and nursery rhymes...magnets, magnifying glasses, seeds, mirrors, containers, and rocks. There are old games (like "Follow the Leader" and "Farmer in the Dell") and new ones that your preschooler or you invent ("let's pretend that..." "what if..." "how many..." or "who will be first to...").

Through your children's play you can learn much about their thoughts and feelings, but don't go too far with that idea. To choose black paint for a picture may indicate fear or sadness—but on the other hand it may be the only color available at the moment! You can also use play activities to help set limits on the really hyperactive youngster and to encourage the one who tends to be withdrawn.

Child's play is important in developing skills, building vocabulary, and solving problems, but it can be a lot of fun, too. Early childhood is a time to think, wonder, learn...and also to be happy.

The Wonderful World of Toys

Toys are very important in the lives of young children. Books, games, and television may take their place as a child grows up, but during the preschool years children need to play with toys.

Too often parents make mistakes in choosing toys. They select ones that they like (rather than the toys a young child can enjoy); that are too big or small, too advanced, or babyish; that don't do anything, so a youngster can have no fun, or that are only educational. A good starting point in selecting toys is to ask, "What can my child do with it?" and "How safe is it?" Also worth asking are the questions, "Will my child like it?" and "What does it teach?"

Some parents give too many toys to their children. (Have you ever seen a three-year-old on Christmas morning with so many that he didn't know which one to try?) Just as serious is the problem of too few. Parents may not know how important toys are, or they may feel that good ones are too expensive.

For young children, toys need not cost much, sometimes nothing at all. A box can become a wagon or a castle. Pieces of cloth can make a rag doll into a princess, and scraps of wood can be piled into a tower. A paper bag can seem like Daddy's lunch pail or briefcase. You provide the parts and children bring the joy of imagination and discovery that makes the toy mean something to them. Dr. Spock once said that "children usually love the simple toys best, and play with them longest." He added, "The small boy pushing a block along a crack on the floor, pretending it's a train, is hard at work learning about the world."

Does your young child have the most basic toys—a ball, a doll (for boys, too), a stuffed animal, and things with which to build, pretend (like a hand puppet), and draw (plus paper and a place to spread it out). You might provide something for your children to make music with, too, remembering that what creates music for little children may not do so for you—pots, pans, and spoons, for example! How much clay and water paints children use depends on the space you have and how well you can control or overlook the mess. Then there are outside toys to sit or climb on, through, or under, to play in (a sandbox or play house, for example), to ride on, and to pull, push, and carry. Because they may be expensive, you might be glad to let your youngster's preschool provide them.

You should sometimes expect a young child to get tired of playing with one toy after a short while, to be awkward in putting things together or piling them up, and to be slow or stubborn in sharing favorite toys with other children. All of that is normal behavior during the early years.

If a toy is to be worthwhile, a child should be able to do something successfully with it—perhaps fit it together, or hug or talk to it. The child should be safe with it, of course. If you check it for sharp points, sharp edges, loudness, and small parts (so easy to swallow or choke on) you might save tears or pain. The age label on the box in which a toy comes may or may not tell you whether your child will enjoy and learn from it. After all, children have different likes and grow up at different rates. There are at least 5,000 new toys each year to choose from, and probably about 150,000 on the market that are made in the United States. If you don't like what the toy teaches, don't buy it. Get something else instead.

Toys can never take the place of your attention and love, of course. But a young child needs them very much. A little television that you watch with your youngster, a few books that you read together, and some simple toys that he plays with alone, side by side with other children, and sometimes with you can all help your child feel good and get ready for the big, complicated world that lies ahead.

Games Children Play

Some years ago (1964 to be exact) Dr. Eric Berne wrote a book called *Games People Play*. It was all about how we manipulate each other, in marriage, on our jobs, and with our friends. We often fall or get pushed into doing things at home, at work, or in social settings because others know what to say or do that will turn us on or off. They can use our strengths and weaknesses for their own purposes.

However, in our adult relationships most of us are actually amateurs. The real experts are our children, who need...our attention and love...and security. That's why they manipulate us. Even in infancy and the preschool years they already know how to get us to do what they wish.

It is not all their doing, of course. We want to turn off their tears and screams, and bring on smiles and laughter. Life is easier for us when they are satisfied. It's fun for us to see them happy. Remember when your preschooler was a baby just a few years ago? Remember how quickly you provided food, a dry diaper, a buggy in motion, or a soft tune to your infant held closely in a rocking chair? You learned something important from such incidents: Offering food, dryness, or attention often turned off the noise. Your baby learned, too; all it took were a few screams to get you to do something pleasant for him.

Now your youngster is older, and even more expert at "playing the game," controlling what you will do for and to her. A young child knows what "buttons to push" to stay up later, see a television show, hear a story, keep the light on, not finish a meal, or make a baby-sitter, older brother or sister—or you—miserable.

Perhaps the complaints will come in words like "I'm tired" or "I'm sick" (so "pay attention to me"), or "I'm lonely" (so "please stay home"). Sometimes tears and whining get the job done for them. "You promised me" may make you feel guilty, or "I'm afraid" (of darkness, thunder, lightning, or "the bogey man") might get your hugs, kisses, and quiet, comforting words.

A young child may only want your sympathy or to get you on his or her side against brothers or sisters. It sometimes takes more wisdom than most of us have to know whether a child is really hurt—or how much of the act is a fake. Many of us do not recognize that our young children spend a lot of time studying us. For many hours, days, and months their major human involvement has been with their parents—what will turn us on or off, what we like and dislike, and how they can get what they want from us. It really makes sense. We are their whole world, so very important in meeting their needs, soothing their fears, solving their problems, and calming their pains. To provide a solution to their cold, dark, wet, hungry, and lonely feelings is our task during these early years. (To cut them loose gracefully, release them from our grasp, cut "the silver cord" is, of course, the main parental job of the later, teen years.)

If a young child can't get our attention through the normal route of tears, questions, and smiles, less acceptable approaches may be used. You know very well what some of the attention-getting approaches are that put a child into newspaper headlines—and into trouble. One of the most frequent childhood "games" is divide-and-conquer, play one parent against the other. In many families the results have been a disaster—arguments between husband or wife at the least, or physical harm to a child, serious disagreements, or even separations at the worst. However, it isn't always so bad to be "manipulated" and "used" by our young children, as long as we know what is going on. After all, most of us enjoy the attention, hugs, and kisses they give us. It may add up to a pretty nice reward to balance some of the problems of parenthood.

Your Young Child's Playmates
(Friends or Enemies?)

Playmates are fun and important to have. They learn from each other and get new ideas and language. Playing alone is sometimes important, too.

Babies are not born with the ability to get along with others. In the early months they seldom even notice another infant. After a year or two they may show their feelings very plainly, by pushing, biting, pulling hair, or grabbing toys. They may play side by side, but not together.

The three-year-old might be ready for closer play, perhaps even for help in a block building, housekeeping, or other project. At four or five, playing together is more common. However, all children are not ready at the same age to be with others.

One of the main changes in the preschool years is the increasing ability to be at ease with other children and adults. But the growth isn't smooth. Calm talking, playing, and working together may take place, of course—but you can still expect some hitting, kicking, and tears. After all, even adult friendships don't always go smoothly. We've just learned to act better toward others than young children sometimes do.

Children often copy what they see in their own families. Those who are part of families that get along well and respect the possessions and privacy of others are likely to be that way toward their playmates. Taking turns (if waiting isn't too long) can be learned at home in connection with which TV show to watch or who rides in the front seat of the family car. You can help your young children get along well with their playmates in many ways:

- Teach them skills, like throwing a ball, riding a tricycle, or using clay and paints. Don't expect them to be very good with them, but they will then be more able to keep up with others.

- Take them places, like to the zoo and to see a bulldozer or crane. Let them help you around the house or on small repair jobs. Then they will be more enjoyable playmates for others.
- Understand that children often want the same toy or wagon at exactly the same time. When it's not used, no one wants it. Such imitating is very common.
- Welcome your child's playmates. Be pleasant but firm with the frequent doorbell-ringer and lunch visitor. Don't yell at or embarrass your children in front of their friends.
- Realize that a child who bullies others is usually unhappy. Showing kindness and an interest in the child, or seeking and correcting the reason for the unhappiness, is important.
- Let your youngster play with one child at a time and for short periods in the early years. Don't assume that your child will always like to be with your friend's children.
- Seek playmates next door or at a nearby park or playground. Young children sometimes need help in finding other small children. Brothers and sisters are fun to have around, but they are not enough.
- Recognize that the best source of friendships (and the professional supervision to go with it) is a well-planned preschool, day-care center, or nursery school.

Parents sometimes don't understand that young children may make friends slowly. Looking at each other, quietly watching, and even playing alone while others are around are all part of the process.

Learning to cooperate takes time, but it doesn't mean that a child should meekly give in. When it's their turn, their toy, or their stuffed animal, even young children should be encouraged to stand up for their rights. That's not the same as being ready to fight. Certain play materials and equipment encourage cooperation (wagons and tricycles, for example). Others are good for playing alone, like simple puzzles, paper, and crayons.

Sometimes a child who had been friendly with others suddenly becomes shy. Perhaps it's because of a new baby in the family—or you've been away, and there is worry that you will be "taken away" again—or you have all moved into a new neighborhood—or there's a separation or divorce or the child has a health, hearing, or sight problem. Talking it over and putting the problem into words, or correcting the health condition, may help turn on the earlier friendliness.

Your goal is quite clear: A child at ease when with others as well as when alone is generally happy and well-adjusted.

The Tooth Fairy, the Easter Bunny, the Stork —and Sweet Dreams

"My wife and I are really at odds on the subject of telling the truth to our children. I think it is a mistake to lie to them, but she feels that 'white lies' are perfectly all right. For example, 'the stork' is very much in her conversations with them—so is 'the tooth fairy.' How can we expect them to tell the truth if we don't? After all, they learn from and copy us."

So wrote a concerned parent…and he is both right and wrong. Parents are the main teachers of their children, more important than any others they have or will have. They do set an example for them, in what they say and how they act. However, it is too bad to deprive a little child of the period of make-believe that exists for such a short while. "The stork" and "the tooth fairy," as well as "the Easter bunny" and the spoken bedtime hope that a child will have "sweet dreams" are obviously imaginary and unreal for adults, but very real, pleasant—and temporary—for most children.

Such thoughts are part of the make-believe life of three-year-olds who pretend they are cars, planes, or animals, and related to the playmates that don't even exist except in the active, fun-loving, play-acting mind of a preschooler. To play house, to pretend to be a space man (or space woman), or to become a firefighter or cowboy for a short, happy time are all involved in growing up. It seems wrong, maybe even cruel, to take them away too fast. A key part of that maturing process are the made-up people and animals related to birth, losing teeth, and celebrating holidays like Christmas and Easter. Without them, much of the glow and glamour of early childhood are missing.

Parents often stimulate their young child's imagination by creating characters in the stories they tell and the games they play together. One family, for example, invented a wise worm called "Timmy Tom" who was very bright, polite (always tipped his hat!), and friendly. He was a bedtime story companion for that quiet time which a little child, as well as parents, can enjoy so much. He was also used for playing counting games, teaching safety rules, and developing a respect for courtesy and someone who is different. Then as the children grew older, he faded away, but he had served many important purposes.

A three-, four-, or five-year-old isn't ready for a fully realistic, descriptive approach to a lost tooth or the birth of a baby. Some of the details can be understood, of course, but what is the hurry to provide more information than a child can understand or absorb? Some parents feel it is necessary to "tell it as it is," with no details omitted. "How are they going to be able to adjust to the pressures of adult life if they don't begin early?" they may ask. Children who are happy and loved will usually adjust easily. They don't need to have every fact provided in full detail...not so early...not until they are ready.

There can be dangers, however, if they always pretend to be a baby, enjoy only the companionship of an imaginary friend, or believe in Santa Claus and all the rest longer than you feel it is healthy to retain such beliefs. You'll probably be able to determine whether and when your youngster is ready to leave behind the happy early years of fantasy and make-believe. No one has to tell the average child after the preschool years that an imaginary playmate doesn't exist, that the spirit of Christmas need not require a "real" Santa Claus, or that dreams are sometimes not "sweet." The child will learn all that in time. But until then let's not take away the fun a little child has in a short-term, unreal world. The real one comes along all too soon.

"What will You be When You Grow Up?"

When a child is small, is it too early to think about how healthy he will be later on? Is it too early to do something to make sure that a growing child will be strong, alert, and happy? No, of course not.

A child's future is very important to parents. However, one part of it is seldom considered. Parents don't often consider what a child will do when she grows up. Perhaps they will when the youngster is older, in elementary or high school through something called "Career Education" for example, but how about during the early years? Should you even think about your young child's future work? What should or can you do about it? Here are some simple, sensible ways to start out, to begin even before your youngster is in school:

- Talk about your work, what your job is, and the people you meet. If you work a full day almost every day, remember that your child doesn't see you for eight or ten hours. What you do during that time is a mystery to the child.
- Give your child just a little information at a time about what you do. Answer questions in words he can understand.
- Ask preschool teachers if they ever visit people at work or invite men and women in to talk about their jobs. Those who work on the local newspaper, at the zoo, or in the gasoline station are often ready to come in. They just have to be asked.
- Offer to go there and tell about your own job. Sit on the floor or on a little chair and talk to the children. Five minutes may be long enough to tell them what you do and why you do it. Tell them the reasons honestly—because you like the work, or it brings in money, for example.

After all, going to nursery school usually costs something, so you work to keep your child there as well as to buy food, clothing, and a place to live. Or—invite them to visit you on the job. Your child will be so proud!

For a long time schools have discussed the subject of "community helpers" (police officers, firefighters, mailcarriers, and a few others). Now we can do a lot more, and earlier. Mothers and fathers have many kinds of jobs. In talking about them, we begin to give young children the idea that some women are doctors, lawyers and, yes, even cab and truck drivers. Some men are nurses, telephone operators, and teachers of young children. We can also give children a picture of the world of work through what they eat, wear, and see.

- How did the bananas, oranges, and chocolate get into our kitchen?
- Who made your shoes, sweater, and hat?
- Who put up that big billboard advertising new cars or homes? Who builds those cars and homes anyway?

All of this may take a little homework on the part of parents, maybe with the help of a good preschool teacher, a nearby librarian, or the encyclopedia.

"Job talk" with young children can easily be overdone, so please be careful. Don't buy toys only because they tie in with some occupation; trucks, nurse kits, and play stoves should be fun, not bought just because they relate to jobs.

You lose some important time in a child's early years if you act as though her future work will never come. It will, sooner than you now think, and helping her see that people do many, many things will begin to open her mind and eyes to what she might someday do.

One government agency publishes a book that lists thousands of jobs. It's unfair to keep a child in the dark about all but the typical "community helpers," plus maybe his doctor and the grocery clerk. If the child hears at least a little bit about what people do to earn a living, the "career education" and school and job decisions that come later on will make more sense. Many of us seldom thought about the job world until we were grown or almost grown. Our young children will perhaps enter it more smoothly if we, once in a while, share with them what we and others do on our jobs.

About the Author

Willard Abraham completed his Ph.D. at Northwestern University, with earlier professional goals at Chicago Teachers College and Illinois Institute of Technology.

His teaching career is still in progress through a successful Copley News Service syndicated column—"Our Children"—and their "For Teens" column. Dr. Abraham has authored 15 books, 127 articles, 5 newspaper columns, 7 special publications, and 83 professional papers and presentations.

Other professional activities have included Captain, U.S. Army Information and Education Division (World War II), Associate Professor at Roosevelt University (Chicago), and Professor of Education and Chairman, Department of Special Education at Arizona State University.

Additional work includes consultant activities for the following: P.F. Collier, Inc., Scholastic, Inc., Sam Rosen Educational Services, Hartley Courseware, Inc., Foundation for Exceptional Children, Bureau of Indian Affairs, Texas Tech Journal of Education, plus sources within Puebla, Mexico, Guam, and Hawaii.

Dr. Abraham enjoys his work, his faculty, and other friends, movies that he has always cherished (if carefully selected), and especially his family: his wife, grown children, and five adorable grandchildren.